101 REASONS
THE
'90s
RULED

M.C. KING

POCKET BOOKS

NEW YORK   LONDON   TORONTO   SYDNEY

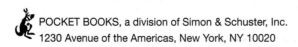

Psychic Friends Network · 98 Marky Mark: rapper & underwe
el · 97 "Studs" (Fox-TV show) · 96 Fashion of the 90s: baby doll dres
mbat boots, cargo pants, Hammerpants · 95 "The Bridges of Madiso
ty" · 94 Vanilla Ice · 93 "Twin Peaks" · 92 Ads of the 90s: Ta
hihuaua, Mentos, Got Milk, Doritos · 91 "Scream" movies · 90 V
n excuse not to get back to someone (pre-cell phone, e-mail). 89 "El
ded on the TV scene, George Clooney became a star 1994 · 88 Arsen
was a fresh, innovative face in late-night (Bill Clinton played sax o
) · 87 John Travolta comeback, Pulp Fiction 1994 · 86 "Xen
or Princess" · 85 RuPaul emerges · 84 We became fascinated wi
Nicole Smith ... ic world by storm
ower Rangers Brown for becomin
gle mother 199 Buzz surroundin
Sixth Sense" 19 77 "Melrose Place
The rise of CDs ntroversy, etc.) · 7
Strug - spraine 8 · 74 "Thelma
e" sparks debat Mouse Club · 7
na's "Truth or " 1995 · 70 Toy
90s · 69 The Lorena / John Wayne Bobbit scandal · 68 Them
rants: Planet Hlwd., All Star Café, Rainforest Café, Fashion Café · 6
mith: from Fresh Prince to movie star · 66 "Saved By The Bell"
er: Iconic coif (Rachel haircut from "Friends") · 65 Susan Lucci win
y, finally, 1999 · 64 Seattle becomes hot — from grunge to Microso
fee · 63 First two seasons of "Ally McBeal" · 62 Fashion of the 90
ercing for men, tattoos not just for bikers anymore · 61 Couples wh
still together: J. Lo & Puff Daddy, Brad & Gwyneth · 60 The Wonderbr
"X-Files" · 58 Y 2 K scare · 57 The "Clueless" phenomenon ("as if"

101 REASONS THE '90s RULED

REASON #101 1993

The Macarena

I t seems like every decade has a dance craze. The '70s had the hustle; the eighties had the Electric Slide; the '90s experienced its first dance phenomenon with la Macarena. Well, actually its second. The first was the Lambada, but we're *forbidden* to talk about that.* Rafael Ruiz and Romero Monge, otherwise known as the duo Los del Rio, recorded the tune in 1993 and released it in their native Spain. Three years later, remixed for dance clubs, it took the English-speaking audience by storm. The U.S. gymnastic team got down to "Ehhh, Macarena" at the 1996 Olympics, as did the Democrats at the National Convention.

* The Lambada was a sexy Brazilian dance whose brief popularity spawned two *Dirty Dancing*–style movies, released on the same day in 1990, respectively titled *Lambada* and *The Forbidden Dance*.

"That was so stupid and great, wasn't it?"

—Julie Brown

"When I dance
they call me
macarena
and the boys they
say that I'm
buena . . ."
—"Macarena"

How to Dance the Macarena

Right arm out, palm down.
Left arm out, palm down.
Right arm out, palm up.
Left arm out, palm up.
Right hand grabs inside of left
  elbow.
Left hand grabs inside of right
  elbow.
Right hand grabs back of neck.
Left hand grabs back of neck.
Right hand on left thigh.
Left hand on right thigh.
Right hand on right butt
  cheek.
Left hand on left butt cheek.
Shake butt to the left.
Shake butt to the right.
Shake butt to the left again.
Quarter turn to the left.
Clap.

REASON #100 1990

Macaulay Culkin Is Home Alone!

A dorable child stars are nothing new, and Macaulay Culkin became the decade's premier kinder-celeb when *Home Alone* hit the big screen. Culkin played Kevin McAllister, a boy whose family accidentally leaves him—you guessed it—home alone while they're vacationing in France. It's *Risky Business* elementary school style with misadventures in shaving and junk-food pig-outs, and then Kevin's house is attacked by hapless burglars. Will Mac survive? Of course! And so will the burglars, played by Joe Pesci and Daniel Stern, who rejoined Mac for 1992's *Home Alone 2: Lost in New York*. None of them returned for *Home Alone 3,* but a little-known youngster did make an appearance: Scarlett Johansson plays Molly, Kevin's little sister.

CHILD STARS OF THE '90s

Kieran Culkin
Jonathan Lipnicki
Jena Malone
Ashley Olsen
Mary-Kate Olsen
Haley Joel Osment
Anna Paquin
Elijah Wood

MACAULAY AFTER *HOME ALONE*

Only the Lonely (1991)

My Girl (1991)

Home Alone 2: Lost in New York (1992)

The Good Son (1993)

The Nutcracker (1993)

Getting Even with Dad (1994)

The Pagemaster (1994)

Richie Rich (1994)

Party Monster (2003)

Saved! (2004)

REASON #99 1990

The Psychic Friends Network

I n 1968, Dionne Warwick won a Grammy for "Do You Know the Way to San José?" In 1990, Dionne found her way onto small screens everywhere as the celebrity spokesperson for the Psychic Friends Network. Want to know what life has in store for you? Dial the 900 number, and at the low, low rate of $3.99 a minute, a *professional* fortune-teller will reveal all. It takes a lot of callers—and a lot of minutes (about 7,500 minutes a day!)—to log more than 100 million dollars a year, but in its heyday the Psychic Friends Network did just that.

"I did call the Psychic Friends Network, but I couldn't get through. So I guess everyone wanted to talk to Dionne Warwick."

—Julie Brown

TOP NAMES IN THE '90s

FOR GIRLS

Ashley
Jessica
Emily
Sarah
Samantha
Brittany
Amanda
Elizabeth
Taylor
Megan
Stephanie
Kayla
Lauren
Jennifer
Rachel
Hannah
Nicole
Amber
Alexis
Courtney

FOR BOYS

Michael
Christopher
Matthew
Joshua
Jacob
Andrew
Daniel
Nicholas
Tyler
Joseph
David
Brandon
James
John
Ryan
Zachary
Justin
Anthony
William
Robert

REASON #98 | 1991

Marky Mark

I n 1991, Mark Wahlberg followed his big brother Donnie of New Kids on the Block fame onto the pop charts with "Good Vibrations," a dance–hip-hop single off the debut album by his band Marky Mark and the Funky Bunch, *Music for the People.* Dropping his drawers at live performances made him famous, and he was hired as an underwear model for Calvin Klein. In 1995, it was good-bye, Marky Mark and those memorable pecs; hello, Mark Wahlberg, serious actor. He abandoned his music career for roles in *Renaissance Man* and *The Basketball Diaries.* And in 1997, Wahlberg hit the big time with a lead role in *Boogie Nights.*

HEARD IN THE '90s

"Did he dazzle you with his extensive knowledge of mineral water, or was it his in-depth analysis of Marky Mark that finally reeled you in? I just would have liked to have been there to watch how you rationalized sleeping with a yuppie-head cheese ball on the first date."

—Troy, *Reality Bites*

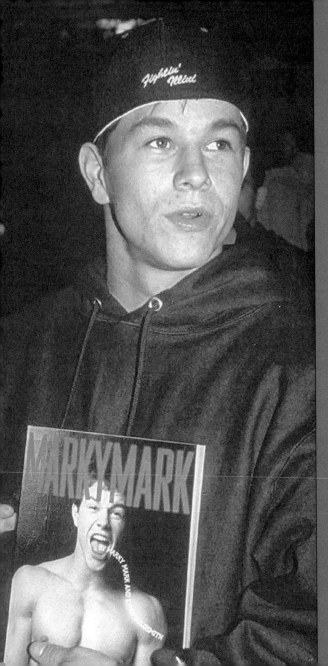

"I'm fortunate I did the things I did. A lot of actors who are very talented still have to feed themselves and pay their bills. But all of that running around in my underwear put a little spending money in my pockets. So, I can just focus on working with good people in interesting movies without having to worry about supporting myself."
—Mark Wahlberg

REASON #97 1991

Studs

T*he Dating Game* ruled from 1965 to 1986. In the '90s, *Studs* ruled. On *Studs,* sexy singles engaged in on-air dating and double entendres like "One trip on those supersonic lips and my runway was ready to take off" and "He's got a butt like a toaster: just ready to pop." With Mark DeCarlo as host (little-known fact: DeCarlo was the biggest prizewinner on another game show, NBC's *Sale of the Century*) the show stayed on the air until 1993.

Studs was so big, *Beverly Hills, 90210* characters Brandon (Jason Priestley) and Steve (Ian Ziering) paid a visit to the show, where they fought over Celeste, played by Jennifer Grant, who later became Steve's on-and-off girlfriend.

During the Los Angeles season of MTV's *The Real World,* Tami was a contestant on *Studs.* Her date was a bust.

SPOTLIGHT ON ...

CHANEL VAMP— 1996

It was deep red with a touch of black and a dash of purple, and it started a revolution in cosmetics. Chanel's VAMP nail polish was the biggest success the company had seen since their signature perfume Chanel No. 5. There were even waiting lists at department-store Chanel counters. The color resembled the deep burgundy Uma Thurman sported on her nails in *Pulp Fiction*. Chanel didn't waste any time building on its success. Soon came Very Vamp, a rich brownish burgundy, then Metallic Vamp, a glittery purple.

HEARD IN THE '90s

Cordelia: Well, you'll be okay here. If you hang with me and mine, you'll be accepted in no time. Of course, we do have to test your coolness factor. You're from L.A., so you can skip the written, but let's see. Vamp nail polish.

Buffy: Um, over?

Cordelia: So over. James Spader.

Buffy: He needs to call me!

Cordelia: Frappaccinos.

Buffy: Trendy, but tasty.

Cordelia: John Tesh.

Buffy: The Devil.

Cordelia: That was pretty much a gimme, but . . . you passed!

Buffy: Oh, goody!

—*Buffy the Vampire Slayer,* Episode 1, 1997

REASON #96

The Baby Doll Dress and Combat Boots

"Baby doll dresses were not flattering. They looked good on babies, but they never really looked great on grown women. But I sure did wear them."
—Jane Pratt, *Jane* magazine

FASHION OF THE '90s

Hey, ladies! Wanna look like it's 1993? Here's what you need:

Runny black eye makeup

Smeared lipstick

Chipped nail polish

Mismatched kids' barrettes

A puffy-sleeved baby doll dress

A pair of black bicycle shorts peeking out from underneath

A tattered cardigan sweater to wear over the dress and/or an old plaid flannel shirt tied around your waist

Black tights—holes not a problem

Doc Martens boots

Legend has it that Doc Martens were the brainchild of a German doctor who injured his foot while skiing in Bavaria. Doc Martens are the orthopedic shoes he designed and are now available in hundreds of colors and styles.

Jennie Garth, fetching in a classic nineties baby doll dress.

15

REASON #95 1992

The Bridges of Madison County

Robert James Waller's romantic novel about a lonely Iowa housewife who has a brief affair with an itinerant *National Geographic* photographer spent three years on the *New York Times* bestseller list, and captured the imaginations of 12 million sappy-hearted readers worldwide. Meryl Streep and Clint Eastwood starred in the hit movie version. Think wistful moments, longing glances, and lots of poignant shots of covered bridges. . . .

THE TOP TEN BESTSELLING BOOKS OF THE '90s

1. *The Pelican Brief,* John Grisham

2. *The Client,* John Grisham

3. *Men Are from Mars, Women Are from Venus: A Practical Guide for Improving Communication and Getting What You Want in Your Relationships,* John Gray

4. *Jurassic Park,* Michael Crichton

5. *The Firm,* John Grisham

6. *In the Kitchen with Rosie: Oprah's Favorite Recipes,* Rosie Daley

7. *The Bridges of Madison County,* Robert James Waller

8. *Rising Sun,* Michael Crichton

9. *The Chamber,* John Grisham

10. *The Runaway Jury,* John Grisham

REASON #94 1990

Vanilla Ice

H is real name was Robert Van Winkle, but Top 40 radio listeners knew him as Vanilla Ice, whose single "Ice Ice Baby" from his debut album *To the Extreme* became a number one hit in 1990. *To the Extreme* sat atop the *Billboard* charts for sixteen weeks, selling more than 7 million copies. But Ice's fame was quick to melt: He confessed to lying about his gangsta past, and many attributed the popularity of his first single to the Queen–David Bowie song from which it liberally sampled. By the time his movie *Cool as Ice* came out in 1991, Ice had no heat.

YO, VIP, LET'S KICK IT!

"All right stop, collaborate and listen
Ice is back with my brand new invention . . ."
        —*"Ice Ice Baby"*

"He was a gorgeous guy. Madonna wanted him. Everyone's ashamed of it now, but they all wanted him."
—Kathy Griffin

REASON #93 1990

Twin Peaks

The tag line was *"A town where everyone knows everyone and nothing is what it seems,"* and for much of 1990 it seemed as if nobody who watched director David Lynch's television series *Twin Peaks* understood *what* was happening on the show—but that didn't keep them from tuning in. Americans were dying to know: Who killed Laura Palmer? Was it the terribly frightening Bob? (Rumor had it that his portrayer wasn't even a real actor, just a creepy-looking crew member.) Or was it her dad, Leland Palmer, of the ever-changing hairstyles? Getting to the bottom of it all was Kyle MacLachlan, as Dale Cooper, the good-hearted FBI agent who really liked to drink coffee and was plagued by nightly visions that involved the murder he was investigating. Lara Flynn Boyle *(The Practice)* played Laura Palmer's best friend, the innocent schoolgirl Donna Hayward; Sherilyn Fenn played Audrey Horne, the not-so-innocent town flirt; and the ubiquitous Laura Palmer was memorably portrayed by Sheryl Lee.

HEARD IN THE '90s

James: When'd you start smokin'?

Donna: I smoke every once in a while. Helps relieve tension.

James: When'd you get so tense?

Donna: When I started smokin'.

—*Twin Peaks*

"*Twin Peaks* is the perfect example of one of those cult shows that made people crazy. The people weren't just fans of the show, they were fanatics."

—Kristen Veitch of E! Online's "Watch with Kristen"

REASON #92

Ads of the '90s

A Doritos commercial that first aired during the 1998 Super Bowl made Ali Laundry—oops! we meant Landry!—a household name. The ad placed the Louisiana native (and former Miss USA) in a Laundromat, where, between loads, she practiced the fine art of catching Doritos in her mouth.

Her real name was Gidget, but we knew her as the distinctly male Taco Bell dog, a pointy-faced Chihuahua with little on its mind but Mexican food. *"Yo quiero Taco Bell"* ("I want some Taco Bell") was the dog's first catchphrase. Next was: "I think I'm in love." (The object of affection: a 99-cent Mexican pizza.) In 1998, he partnered with Godzilla: "Here, lizard, lizard, lizard," beckoned the dog. The Chihuahua was not without detractors, as Hispanic groups accused the ad campaign of promoting demeaning stereotypes. But the Chihuahua endured, becoming a product itself: In the late '90s, Taco Bell dog plush toys and paraphernalia flooded the stores. The dog's last big slogan was "Woo, drop the chalupa!" But in 2000, Taco Bell dropped the Chihuahua.

Gidget appeared in the 1999 film *Crazy in Alabama,* starring Melanie Griffith and directed by Antonio Banderas.

Gidget had understudies named Dinky and Taco.

REASON #91

The *Scream* Movies

What do you get when you cross *A Nightmare on Elm Street* with *Dawson's Creek? Scream,* a meta horror flick whose tongue-in-cheek plotting thrilled slasher fans and semiotics majors alike. Also, the movie featured lots of hot young actors. *Party of Five*'s Neve Campbell played Sidney, a high-school student who's being stalked by her mother's murderer. *Friends* star Courteney Cox portrayed an aggressive tabloid reporter. Skeet Ulrich was Campbell's boyfriend, David Arquette the bumbling deputy sheriff. Add Drew Barrymore, Rose McGowan, and Jamie Kennedy to the mix, and you've got a mega-franchise. In the years to come we also had *Scream 2* (1997) and *Scream 3* (2000).

SCARY MOVIES OF THE '90s

1996, 1997, 2000 *Scream 1–3*

1991
The Silence of the Lambs

1993
Jurassic Park

1997
The Lost World: Jurassic Park

1999
The Sixth Sense

1999
The Mummy

1999
The Blair Witch Project

1998
Godzilla

1997
Alien: Resurrection

REASON #90

The Cell Phone

- In 1995, the average per-minute rate for a cell phone call was **56 cents.**

- In 1997, a wireless phone cost, on average, about **$132.**

- The first truly iconic cell phone design was Motorola's StarTAC that resembled a clamshell and was available in several colors.

- In 1993, the average cell phone weighed **2 pounds;** now they weigh 2 ounces.

- By the end of the '90s, about **24 percent** of American girls owned a cell phone.

- Remember the days when people couldn't track you down no matter where you were? Neither can we.

Can you believe cell phones were ever that big?

REASON #89

ER

The hour-long drama about life in a Chicago hospital's emergency room, conceived by former medical student and *Jurassic Park* author Michael Crichton, hit the air with a two-hour pilot on September 19, 1994. Critics and viewers immediately took note of the show's uniquely frenetic energy, in-your-face camera work, and charismatic cast. Anthony Edwards played Dr. Mark Greene, a world-class physician. Noah Wyle took the role of Dr. John Carter, a med student continually bumping up against his mentor, Dr. Peter Benton (played by Eriq La Salle); Julianna Margulies was the compassionate Nurse Carol Hathaway, struggling to get over her turbulent romance with the ravishing pediatrician in residence, George Clooney's Dr. Doug Ross.

Until *ER,* Clooney had been a regular working actor with small roles on *The Facts of Life* and *Roseanne.* With *ER,* his star skyrocketed, and a career on the big screen began to flourish: in the late '90s, Clooney starred as Seth Gecko in *From Dusk Till Dawn,* as Batman in *Batman & Robin,* and as criminal mastermind Jack Foley in *Out of Sight.* (To name just a few . . .) He left *ER* after the fifth season, returning for a "surprise" appearance a year later when Margulies bid the series adieu.

On September 25, 1997, *ER* made television history, broadcasting the night's episode live—twice (first for East Coast viewers, then for the West Coast). There were only a few small glitches, and the double airing made for some interesting inconsistencies. For instance, Clooney's character was watching a baseball game in live time, but the baseball scores were different for each airing.

"*ER* opened big and never looked back. The movement of the camera, the urgency to that show was so great, the audience said: 'This is it, this is television like we've never seen it before.'"

—Warren Littlefield, former head of programming, NBC

REASON #88

Arsenio Hall

*T*he *Arsenio Hall Show* debuted just as the '80s were ending and remained on the air for the first half of the '90s. The first successful late-night talk show to be hosted by a person of color, *The Arsenio Hall Show* scored demographics the other late-night shows had trouble reaching: namely young, urban, African American and Latino viewers. Hall didn't have a desk or a sidekick, but he did have the "dog pound"—a group of rowdy guests sitting near the band, who cried, "Woof! Woof! Woof!" and pumped their arms in the air. The show scored with a guest appearance by presidential hopeful Bill Clinton, who played two songs on his saxophone on a 1992 show. And Magic Johnson chose *The Arsenio Hall Show* as the place to visit after he announced to the world that he was HIV positive.

"I came to Hollywood with this mission, this dream, and it all came true."

—Arsenio Hall

REASON #87 1995

Xena: Warrior Princess

I t was a *Hercules* spin-off, only this time it was buffed-out babes wearing the breast-plates. *Xena: Warrior Princess,* an hour-long action-filled drama, debuted in 1995 and went on to enormous syndication success. Xena (Lucy Lawless) is a reformed outlaw, who works out her guilt by trampling the Greek countryside with her gal pal Gabrielle in pursuit of bad guys—think barbarian half-wits and nefarious demigods.

ALSO IN 1995 . . .

The Atlanta Braves win the World Series.

"It was the '90s zeitgeist, the reemergence of the female hero."

—Lucy Lawless

HEARD IN THE '90s

Gabrielle: Another one's fallen for you.

Xena: Again? What is it?

Gabrielle: Oh, the blue eyes . . . the leather. Men love leather.

Xena: I think it's time for a wardrobe change.

—*Xena: Warrior Princess*

REASON #86 | 1994

Pulp Fiction

Quentin Tarantino's hipster homage to violence featured splattered brains, stylized dancing, and lots of retro gangster posturing. It also resuscitated the lagging career of '70s movie icon John Travolta. Travolta and Samuel L. Jackson play hit men; Bruce Willis is an aging boxer; Ving Rhames is a mob boss; Uma Thurman, Rhames's wife in need of a good night on the town. The film won the Palme d'Or at the Cannes Film Festival, and grossed more than 200 million worldwide. It also spawned a slew of imitators that never quite topped the original.

"Pulp Fiction was great—getting a shot in the heart never looked so appealing."
—Laura Kightlinger

HEARD IN THE '90s

Vincent: You know what they call a Quarter Pounder with cheese in Paris?

Jules: They don't call it a Quarter Pounder with cheese?

Vincent: No, man, they got the metric system, they don't know what the fu** a Quarter Pounder is.

Jules: What do they call it?

Vincent: They call it a Royale with cheese.

Jules: Royale with cheese.

Vincent: That's right.

Jules: What do they call a Big Mac?

Vincent: Big Mac's a Big Mac, but they call it Le Big Mac.

Jules: Le Big Mac. What do they call a Whopper?

Vincent: I don't know. I didn't go into Burger King.

—Pulp Fiction

REASON #85 1992

RuPaul

In 1992 a six-foot-five (some say six-foot-seven) drag queen named RuPaul Andre Charles—*with a name like that, how could he be anything but a star?*—found his way onto the *Billboard* charts with the dance hit "Supermodel," a tribute to working the runway, diva style. "I've got one thing to say," went the song, "sashay, shante, shante, shante!" But RuPaul had a lot more to say—and thankfully, most of it made a lot more sense than that. As the premier *out* celeb-rity, RuPaul forged a path for gay entertainers and sent a message of love to anyone who'd listen: "If you don't love yourself, how the hell you gonna love somebody else?" RuPaul blazed his way through the decade, becoming the first drag queen to become a cosmetics spokesperson for M.A.C. cosmetics, penning an autobiography, the aptly titled *Letting It All Hang Out,* and hosting a talk show on VH1.

> **HEARD IN THE '90s**
>
> "You better work, bitch!"
> —RuPaul

> "RuPaul was like the Frankenstein of drag queens who was made from the parts of superstars: Cher's attitude, Diana Ross's hair, Tina Turner's legs. . . ."
> —Michael Musto

SUPER-MODELS WHO REIGNED IN THE '90s

Linda Evangelista

Naomi Campbell

Christy Turlington

Kate Moss

Shalom Harlow

Cindy Crawford

Amber Valletta

Heidi Klum

Elle Macpherson

Veronica Webb

Tyra Banks

REASON #84 1993

Anna Nicole

She may not have qualified as a supermodel, but in 1993, *Playboy Playmate* turned Guess? jeans model Anna Nicole Smith became the poster girl for frat houses across the country. In 1994, she broke the hearts of legions of American men when she married billionaire oil tycoon J. Howard Marshall II, who was eighty-nine years old. He died fourteen months later. Legal battles and weight gain ensued . . . and we couldn't stop watching.

ALSO IN 1993 . . .

The New Kids on the Block retire.

REASON #83 | 1998

Britney Spears

On November 30, 1998, Jive Records released the first single off a new teenybopper's album. Her name was Britney Spears, the song was " . . . Baby One More Time," and the album was, appropriately enough, . . . *Baby One More Time.* At seventeen years old, Britney Spears became the youngest recording artist to have a first single debut at number one on the *Billboard* Hot 100, and . . . *Baby One More Time* became the biggest-selling album by a teenager.

ALSO IN 1993 . . .

Mark McGwire and Sammy Sosa break Roger Maris's single season homerun record.

REASON #82

Mighty Morphin Power Rangers

Here's the premise: Zordon, an interdimensional creature, empowers five attitudinal teenagers with the ability to morph into superheroes in order to protect the world from the evil space-witch Rita Repulsa and her minions, who want to take over the earth. Zordon is like Charlie of *Charlie's Angels,* though viewers do get to see him—he's a holograph, and all head. His teenage recruits are trained in martial arts, which they employ when they aren't summoning the giant transforming robots, known as Zords. Or something like that . . .

FUN FACT

Amy Jo Johnson, aka Julie from *Felicity*, played Kimberly, the first Pink Power Ranger.

REASON #81 1992

Dan Quayle vs. Murphy Brown

"**B**earing babies irresponsibly is, simply, wrong. Failure to support children one has fathered is wrong. We must be unequivocal about this. It doesn't help matters when prime time TV has Murphy Brown—a character who supposedly epitomizes today's intelligent, highly paid, professional woman—mocking the importance of a father, by bearing a child alone, and calling it just another 'lifestyle choice.' I know it is not fashionable to talk about moral values, but we need to do it. Even though our cultural leaders in Hollywood, network TV, the national newspapers routinely jeer at them, I think that most of us in this room know that some things are good, and other things are wrong. Now it's time to make the discussion public."

Murphy Brown writers responded to then Vice President Dan Quayle's disparaging remarks about their character's decision to become a single parent with a two-part season opener called "You Say Potatoe, I Say Potato," which mocked the veep for correcting a New Jersey elementary student's "misspelling" of the word "potato." (Quayle told the tot it was "potatoe.") The episode ended with a Dumpster of potatoes being delivered to the White House. Quayle and his boss George H. W. Bush were not reelected that November.

"If Mr. Quayle feels that single parenthood is immoral and that a woman cannot adequately raise a child by herself, then he should see to it that abortion remains safe and legal in this country."

—Diane English, creator of *Murphy Brown*

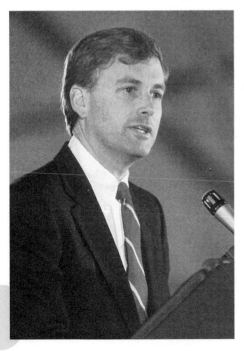

" . . . I love football and potato chips, so this was a natural. Potatoes have become a big part of my life, but this time I'm enjoying them!"

—Dan Quayle in 1994, when he appeared in a commercial for Lay's potato chips

45

REASON #80

American Gladiators

From 1989 until 1997, Fox's take on the ancient Roman sporting event captured the public's imagination and quenched a curious thirst for barbaric behavior. The hour-long competition—Think *Battle of the Network Stars* meets WWF or *Captain Caveman* meets *Scooby's All-Star Laff-A-Lympics,* only with real live people—starred oiled-up muscle-bound competitors named Nitro, Elektra, Turbo, and Viper and featured events like Joust, Human Cannonball, Hang Tough, and Powerball. Spandex and smack talk were the show's hallmarks, and a bevy of ancillary products from candy bars to trading cards to Nintendo games rounded out the phenomenon.

"There's something sexy about an incredibly blonde woman named Ice with a giant Q-tip, ready to take you on."

—Joel Stein, columnist

REASON #79 1999

The Sixth Sense

Bruce Willis gets sensitive and kid star Haley Joel Osment "sees dead people" in this supernatural thriller written and directed by M. Night Shyamalan. The movie's tagline may have been "Not every blessing is a gift," but this flick was blessed with six Oscar nominations (including one for preteen Osment) and roughly $600 million in worldwide box office returns. The surprise ending was the subject of water cooler chatter for months, and Shyamalan established himself as one of Hollywood's most exciting new filmmakers. (Bruce's career got a nice boost, too.)

"I see dead people."
—Cole

47

REASON #78 1999

Ricky Martin

Before 'N Sync 'n spawned Justin Timberlake, there was another boy-band prodigy who mesmerized a nation of teens and tweens. He was Ricky Martin, né Enrique José Martín Morales IV, who at thirteen was the lead singer of the premier boy band of the early '80s, Menudo. In 1994, Ricky briefly joined the cast of *General Hospital*, a veritable breeding ground for musical superstuds. (Rick Springfield and Jack Wagner, anyone?) After a stint on Broadway in megahit *Les Misérables* and four hit records in Spanish, Martin released his first English-language pop album. He soon had all of America "livin' la vida loca," and shaking their bon-bons. Thanks to his wild popularity, he shebanged himself all the way to *el banco*. . . .

ALSO IN 1999 . . .

The Pashmina becomes popular.

"He was purely sexy, purely charismatic, oh so confident and fine, all you could do was say 'Thank God for men!' You talk about *caliente*. *¡Este hombre!*"
—Sheryl Lee Ralph

49

REASON #77

Melrose Place

A spin-off of *Beverly Hills, 90210,* this Darren Star–Aaron Spelling nighttime sudster about a group of twenty-somethings who lived in a West Hollywood apartment complex got off to a tame start. The cast featured dull-witted Allison, who just wanted to succeed at her job at an ad agency; dreary Billy, who wanted to be the great American novelist; soft-spoken Doug; Jake, the tough-guy heartthrob; Rhonda, who was looking for love; and the resident married couple, Dr. Michael and Jane Mancini.

Life on Melrose started to heat up when Heather Locklear joined the cast, playing ruthless ad executrix Amanda. Producers injected some serious pathos into the scripts by introducing Jane's manipulative little sister, Sydney—the apartment complex's very own Heidi Fleiss—and turned Michael into a wicked sociopath. And don't forget Marcia Cross as the deranged Dr. Kimberly Shaw! The moment when Kimberly tears off her wig to reveal her surgery-scarred skull stands as one of the most memorable shockers in nighttime soap history.

TEST YOUR *MELROSE* KNOW-HOW

Can you match the cast member to the character he or she played?

ACTOR		CHARACTER	
1	Linden Ashby	a	Brooke Armstrong Campbell
2	Josie Bissett	b	Ryan McBride
3	Thomas Calabro	c	Dr. Brett Cooper
4	David Charvet	d	Sandy Louise Harling
5	Marcia Cross	e	Victoria "Taylor" Davis McBride
6	Kristin Davis	f	Kyle McBride
7	Rob Estes	g	Dr. Michael Mancini
8	Brooke Langton	h	Amanda Woodward
9	Laura Leighton	i	Megan Lewis Mancini McBride
10	Amy Locane	j	Dr. Peter Burns
11	Heather Locklear	k	Jane Andrews Mancini
12	Jamie Luner	l	Matt Fielding
13	Alyssa Milano	m	Samantha Reilly Campbell
14	John Haymes Newton	n	Rhonda Blair
15	Lisa Rinna	o	Craig Field
16	Kelly Rutherford	p	Jake Hanson
17	Doug Savant	q	Sydney Andrews Field Mancini
18	Grant Show	r	Lexi Sterling
19	Andrew Shue	s	Dr. Kimberly Shaw
20	Courtney Thorne-Smith	t	Billy Campbell
21	Jack Wagner	u	JoBeth Reynolds
22	Vanessa Williams	v	Jennifer Mancini
23	Daphne Zuniga	w	Allison Parker

ANSWERS: 1c, 2k, 3g, 4o, 5s, 6a, 7f, 8m, 9q, 10d, 11h, 12r, 13v, 14b, 15e, 16i, 17l, 18p, 19j, 20w, 21t, 22n, 23u.

REASON #76

The Rise of CDs

IMPORTANT DATES IN CD HISTORY

1990   **28%** of all U.S. households have CD players.

1992   CDs outsell cassette tapes for the **first time ever.**

1992   Sony releases the Mini-Disc.

1993   The Recording Industry Association of America puts a stop to packaging CD in cumbersome cardboard packages because of environmental waste.

1997   **DVDs** and DVD players hit the consumer market.

REASON #75 1996

Kerri Strug

A tlanta, July 23, 1996: the last day of competition for the women's gymnastic Olympic team; the United States has secured a silver medal, and has only a slim hope for the gold. That hope rests on the teeny-tiny shoulders of the final vaulter in the competition, diminutive eighteen-year-old Arizona native Kerri Strug. But in her first vault, Strug falls—hard!—tearing two ligaments and spraining her left ankle. Still, she attempts the second vault, and does it magnificently, nailing an almost perfect landing before collapsing in a heap of pain. USA wins the gold; Strug becomes famous for being carried triumphantly in the arms of proud Coach Bela Karolyi; and then later fulfills the dreams of teens everywhere by landing a cameo with heartthrob Brian Austin Green on *Beverly Hills, 90210.*

RANDOM FACTS ABOUT KERRI STRUG

She's Jewish!

She has a really REALLY high voice!

You can hire her as a motivational speaker!

REASON #74 1991

Thelma & Louise

Thelma and Louise are friends.
Thelma and Louise go on a road trip.
Thelma and Louise stop at a bar.
A guy harasses Thelma.
He threatens to rape Thelma!
Louise shoots the guy.
Thelma and Louise are upset.
Thelma and Louise are invigorated.
Thelma and Louise start breaking laws left and right.
Thelma and Louise rob a convenience store!
Thelma and Louise put a cop in the trunk of a car!
Thelma has liberating sex with a really hot guy.
He turns out to be a con man!
The cops are after Thelma and Louise!
Thelma and Louise get caught.
Except they decide to keep going. . . .
For Thelma and Louise, liberation comes at a really big price.

"What I loved most about *Thelma & Louise* is that they left room for a sequel."

—Jeremy Kramer, comedian

HEARD IN THE '90s

Thelma: Let's not get caught.

Louise: What are you talking about?

Thelma: Let's keep going.

—*Thelma & Louise*

"I liked that movie, because it was a movie about friendship and about love and women coming together and I think it really showed men that we're crazy. We're really crazy. Just try us."

—Sherri Shepherd, *Less Than Perfect*

REASON #73

MMC

Who needs The Juilliard School? In the '90s, there was no better breeding ground for talent than Disney Channel's *MMC. The Mickey Mouse Club* first became a staple of squeaky-clean kiddy TV in 1955. It was remade as *The New Mickey Mouse Club* in the '70s. But the third time's the charm, and *MMC,* the '90s incarnation of the variety show, had a way with the budding celebs. Donning mouse ears, participating in hilariously funny skits, and warming up their vocal cords were future pop stars Britney Spears, Justin Timberlake, "JC" Chasez, and Christina Aguilera, as well as future actors Keri Russell and Ryan Gosling. Take that, Annette Funicello!

SPOTLIGHT ON . . .
CALLER ID

Caller ID is to the '90s what call-waiting was to the '80s: the kind of innovation you can't imagine ever having lived without. How can it be that there was ever a time you didn't know who was calling before picking up the phone???

In 1995, caller ID became available nationwide in the United States. At first you had to buy a caller ID box to track your calls. Now it's the most popular add-on feature in land-line telephone services, and is featured on almost all wireless phones.

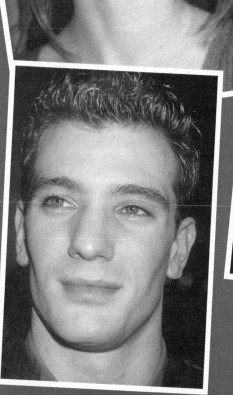

REASON #72 1992

Madonna: Truth or Dare

Filmmaker Alek Keshishian's documentary film about Madonna's 1990 Blond Ambition tour (the one with the Jean Paul Gaultier cone breasts) was a behind-the-scenes romp in which Madonna played parlor games with her dancers; got per-snickety with her hairdresser as well as then boyfriend Warren Beatty; made fun of Kevin Costner for calling her show "neat"; and waxed melancholy about her family and her lost love, Sean Penn. Today, in the age of reality television, exposing that much would seem de rigueur; in 1991, it was cutting edge—and downright scandalous.

> "A behind-the-scenes look at what we'd never seen before. You saw self-pleasuring on stage, you saw nudity backstage; you saw Madonna in a prayer circle with her dancers before the show and then she ends up with the dancers after the show."
>
> —Molly Mayock, film critic

HEARD IN THE '90s

"Why say anything if it's not on camera?"
—Warren Beatty, in *Madonna: Truth or Dare*

"It was a bunch of future stars all doing their best, kookiest, most outrageous work. There were funny skits with U2 as the Partridge Family, Bruce Springsteen leaving a phone message, crazy stuff. Sounds weird, was weird, and was truly ahead of its time."

—Michael Musto

REASON #71 1992

The Ben Stiller Show

B en Stiller's sketch comedy show starring then unknowns Janeane Garafalo, Andy Dick, and Bob Odenkirk attracted a wide range of guest stars—from Isabel Sanford of *The Jeffersons* fame to Gary Coleman from *Diff'rent Strokes* to Sarah Jessica Parker and Roseanne Barr. Judd Apatow (*The Larry Sanders Show, Freaks and Geeks*) and David Cross (*Arrested Development, Mr. Show*) were credited as writers. Despite the talented acting and writing teams, the show didn't win in the ratings game, and was on the air for only twelve episodes before Fox gave it the ax. Ironically, it was nominated for six Emmys and won one (Outstanding Achievement in Writing in a Variety or Music Program) just after being canceled.

ALSO IN 1992 . . .

The Nicoderm Patch hits the market.

REASON #70 1996

Tickle Me Elmo

C hristmas, 1996: A red and fuzzy plush toy in the likeness of the *Sesame Street* star Tickle Me Elmo had parents mauling each other in the aisles of Toys "R" Us. There was such a demand for the toy, rumor had it that by late December, consumers were shelling out upwards of $2,500.00 for the doll. Not bad, considering it retailed for under $40.

Tickle Me Elmo was such a success, he's credited with invigorating the overall plush toy market. In 1997, Tyco Toys gave Elmo some giggly pals, and Tickle Me Cookie Monster and Tickle Me Big Bird hit the market.

OTHER HOT TOYS OF THE '90s

FURBY: Two years later, America fell in love with a plush toy a little more exotic than Elmo: his name was Furby; he spoke the language Furbish (*ah-may koh koh* means "Pet me more"); he sneezed and giggled; and he was battery operated. In just over a year, there were 12 million Furbys sold worldwide—and that was before he went electronic!

POKÉMON: Short for "Pocket Monster," a Japanese video game that became a card game that led to an animated TV series and then movies that made no sense to anyone over the age of ten.

RANDOM TOY FACTS

• In 1992 a new Barbie doll entered the market. Her name was Teen Talk Barbie, and it didn't take long for her to put her perfectly arched foot in her mouth. Among her small repertoire of sayings were: "I love shopping," "Meet me at the mall," and "Math class is tough." Mothers and math mavens alike screamed foul, accusing Barbie of promoting stereotypes.

• Beanie Babies hit the market in 1993, and by 1996 had sold 100 million units. That number skyrocketed when Beanie Babies teamed up with McDonald's, and you could get a little stuffed critter with your Happy Meal.

• In 1997, Mattel, Inc.'s Share A Smile® Becky® was the first fashion doll who used a wheelchair.

REASON #69 1993

The
Lorena and John Wayne
Bobbitt
Scandal

"Lorena Bobbitt scared the hell out of a lot of men. I think she basically did for dating what *Jaws* did for swimming in the ocean."

—Vance DeGeneres writer and producer

In 1993, Virginia manicurist Lorena Bobbitt boldly went where other women had only fantasized about going before. First into the knife drawer, then into her bedroom, where she cut off the penis of her sleeping husband, John Wayne Bobbitt. Lorena was found not guilty on the grounds that she had experienced an "irresistible impulse" to cut off her husband's penis and was not liable for her actions. She was committed to a mental health facility for observation. Meanwhile, John Wayne Bobbitt parlayed his cutting-edge status into minor celebrity. After a nine-hour reattachment surgery, he appeared in the porn movies *Frankenpenis* and *John Wayne Bobbitt Uncut.* In 1997, Bobbitt moved to Nevada, where he became a minister in a Las Vegas church.

Theme Restaurants

"Who ever decided that restaurants should not be about food and they should be about Hollywood?"

—Jane Pratt

"The Fashion Café? Who was eating?"
—Sheryl Lee Ralph

REASON #67 1990

Will Smith

*T*he *Fresh Prince of Bel-Air* aired on NBC from 1990 to 1996, morphing rapper Will Smith into a TV star. A meaty role in the 1993 film adaptation of John Guare's *Six Degrees of Separation* marked Smith as movie material, and by 1995 he was starring in blockbuster action flicks. First there was *Bad Boys,* a buddy picture with Martin Lawrence, then *Independence Day, Men in Black* and *Wild Wild West.* With the release of *Men in Black,* Smith relaunched his music career as a solo artist with the mega hit—wait for it—"Men in Black." In 1997 he broke the hearts of women everywhere when he married actress Jada Pinkett, although they made such a cute couple that it was hard to remain bitter.

HEARD IN THE '90s

"I go psycho when my new joint hit

Just can't sit, gotta get jiggy wit it. . . ."

—Will Smith, "Gettin' Jiggy Wit It"

REASON #66

Saved by the Bell

For kids growing up in the early '90s, Saturday mornings were reserved for slurping down sugary cereal with their pals at Bayside High School—otherwise known as Zack, Slater, Screech, Lisa, Kelly, and Jessie—from NBC's *Saved by the Bell*. Wacky high jinks, dumb puns, and practical jokes on the nitwit principal, Mr. Belding, made the show a super cute escape from reality. The super cute stars—namely leads Tiffani-Amber Thiessen, Elizabeth Berkley, and Mark-Paul Gosselaar—didn't hurt either. When the stars aged, NBC developed a prime-time vehicle for the ensemble, *Saved by the Bell: The College Years*. There were also TV movies—*Saved by the Bell: Hawaiian Style* and *Saved by the Bell: Wedding in Las Vegas*—to capitalize on the craze. And, lest Saturday-morning viewers be left in the dust, NBC put *Saved by the Bell: The New Class* in its predecessor's time slot. *The New Class* stayed on the air for the rest of the decade.

There was life after high school for most of the stars of *Saved by the Bell*. Tiffani-Amber Thiessen joined the cast of *Beverly Hills, 90210,* and then *Two Guys, a Girl, and a Pizza Place.* Mark-Paul Gosselaar starred in *NYPD Blue*. Mario López became a talk-show host. Elizabeth Berkley made history starring in the decade's campiest classic, *Showgirls* And Dustin Diamond, aka Screech, kept the legend going in *Saved by the Bell: The New Class*.

"My inner child is Screech, so I'm a Screech gal. I think Screech has it going on, as they would say in the nineties."

—Kathy Griffin

REASON #65 | 1999

Susan Lucci Wins the Emmy!

Nominated nineteen times for best actress in a daytime drama for playing Erica Kane on ABC's *All My Children*, Lucci ends her losing streak and finally takes a trophy home. Las Vegas oddsmakers weep with joy.

REASON #64

Seattle

Starbucks, grunge music, Microsoft, Frasier Crane . . . What do these things have in common? They all hail from Seattle, the capital of the Northwest, a movie locale of choice (think *Sleepless in Seattle* and *Singles*), and the hippest—or at least most hyped—city of the early '90s. So what if it rains a lot?

HEARD IN THE '90s

"So, okay, I don't wanna be a traitor to my generation and all, but I don't get how guys dress today. I mean, c'mon, it looks like they just fell outta bed and put on some baggy pants and take their greasy hair and cover it up with a backwards cap and like we're expected to swoon? I don't think so."

—Cher Horowitz, *Clueless*

REASON #63 | 1997

Ally McBeal

Television is no stranger to perky single gals, and in 1997, Ally McBeal joined the ranks of Mary Richards and Rhoda Morgenstern, and *That Girl*'s Ann Marie in an hourlong comedy created and produced by *LA LAW*'s David E. Kelley. Wispy Calista Flockhart starred as Ally, a neurotic Boston attorney looking for love. In terms of personality, Ally had an edge on her predecessors—she occasionally seemed more disturbed than quirky, prone to visual and auditory hallucinations. For example, she made peace with her biological clock by befriending an imaginary dancing baby, and received relationship counsel from an hallucination of Al Green.

Ally's behavior and wardrobe raised plenty of eyebrows, prompting an infamous *Time* magazine cover to pose the question, "Is feminism dead?" That didn't stop young women from tuning in to the show in droves. And Calista Flockhart eventually hooked up with Harrison Ford offscreen, so she must have been doing *something* right.

"Whenever I get depressed, I raise my hemlines. If things don't change, I am bound to be arrested."

—Ally McBeal

REASON #62

FASHION OF THE '90s

Body Art

- Roseanne Barr got a tattoo that read, "Property of Tom Arnold." When they broke up, Arnold jibed that that "made him the fourth-largest property owner in California."

- Pamela Anderson and Tommy Lee got matching tattooed wedding bands.

- In 1997, the Associated Press reported that 35.1% of all NBA players had tattoos.

- For those who wanted their body art less permanent, there were henna tattoos, Celtic body art, and bindhis like those sported by Madonna and Gwen Stefani.

"Tattoos are like stories—they're symbolic of the important moments in your life. Sitting down, talking about where you got each tattoo and what it symbolizes, is really beautiful."

—Pamela Anderson

REASON #61

Celebrity Couples

B ack in the days of yore, before celebrity couples were clamoring to expose their relationships for reality-TV cameras, there were dazzling duos who still tried to act like they didn't know what the fuss was all about. The '90s had its share: Woody and Soon-Yi . . . Pamela and Tommy . . . Will and Jada . . . But the most sun-dappled couple of the '90s got together on the set of the movie *Se7en*. They were Brad Pitt and Gwyneth Paltrow, and, after a whirlwind courtship spent dodging meddlesome paparazzi, they announced their engagement. That was the end of 1996. Half a year later, they'd broken up and moved on: she to Ben Affleck; he to Jennifer Aniston.

It's hard to imagine a time when Jennifer Lopez *needed* publicity, but back in the late '90s, some people said that was the only reason she was dating rap megastar P. Diddy, then known as Puff Daddy. Puff and Jen made for an eye-catching pair, and it sure looked like real love. Then, in 1999, the couple witnessed a shoot-out at a nightclub, and he was charged with bribery and illegal possession of a firearm, but was acquitted in 2001. Jen stood by him—but only for a while. The two called it quits even before Puff was cleared.

"They were too
blonde to stay
together . . . They
just canceled each
other out."
—Julie Brown

"It was a simpler
time back in the
'90s. P. Diddy was
still Puff Daddy or
Puffy. He was still
with J. Lo, who was
still Jennifer Lopez."
—Vance DeGeneres

REASON #60 1994

The Wonderbra

The year 1994 marked the auspicious U.S. debut of the Wonderbra, a padded push-up bra that was already a hit in England. It lifted, separated, and gave the illusion of ample cleavage. According to the manufacturer, in its first year on the market, U.S. sales moved "at a rate of one Wonderbra every fifteen seconds." A massive ad campaign featured comely model Eva Herzigova and the slogan, "Look me in the eyes and tell me that you love me." The bra signaled the return of the shapely figure and the end of the waif trend. Kate Moss, the English model who popularized the waif look, claimed that the Wonderbra gave even her some cleavage.

"Wonderbra has a lot to do, in my estimation, with false advertising. You take a girl home, she takes off her bra, and her breasts go with it."

—Danny Bonaduce

"I think girls should just get Wonderbras and not get boob jobs."
—Kathy Griffin

ALSO IN 1994...

Los Angeles suffers a major earthquake.

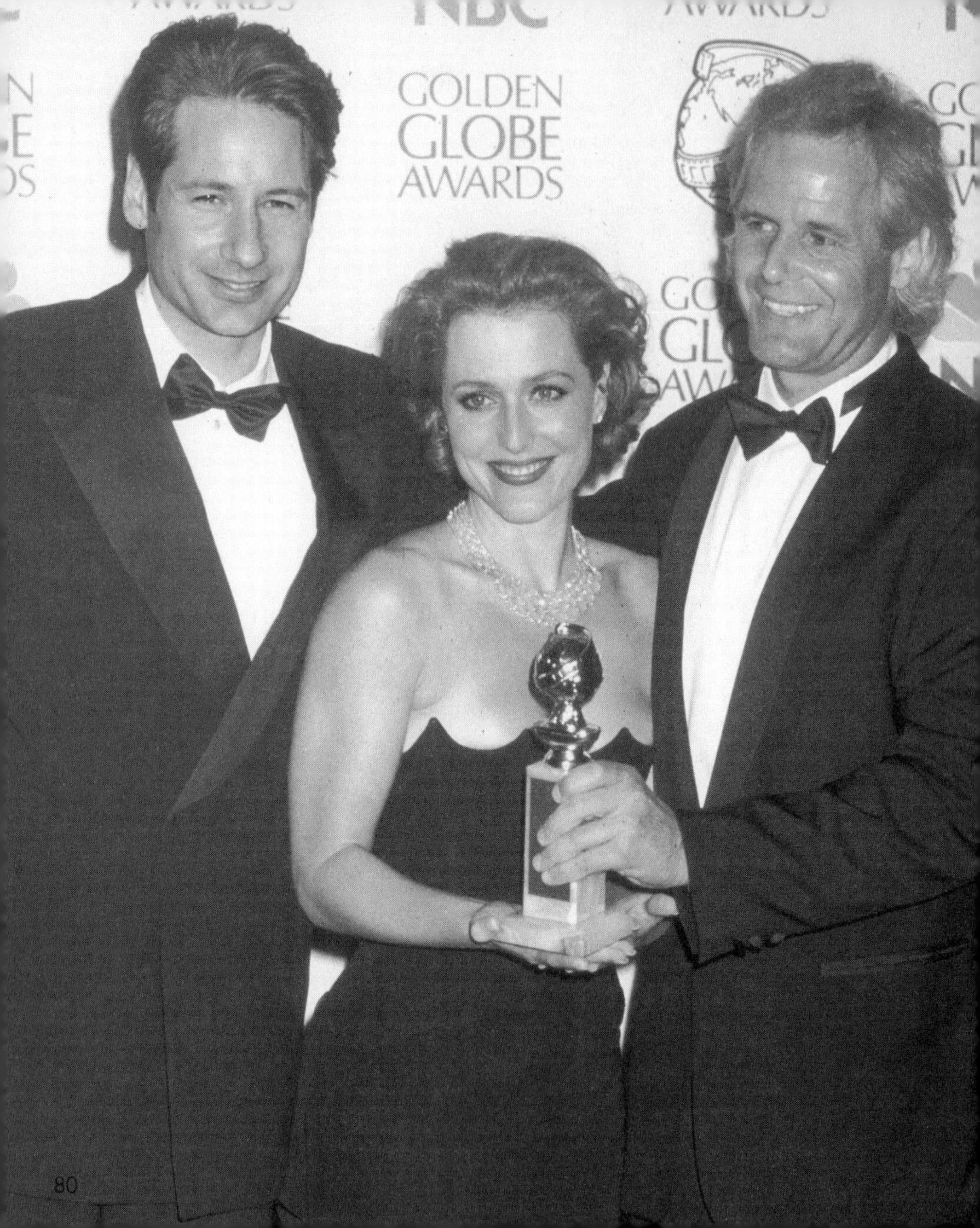
NBC
GOLDEN
GLOBE
AWARDS

REASON #59 1993

The X-Files

Beginning in 1993, sci-fi wasn't (exclusively) for nerds anymore. In this groundbreaking cult TV hit, David Duchovny and Gillian Anderson played Fox Mulder and Dana Scully, unnaturally good-looking FBI investigators of the paranormal, who encountered UFOs, deceptive government agents, and oodles of sexual tension. Obsessive fans called "X-Philes" helped keep Mulder and Scully at the forefront of the pop culture zeitgeist—and a force to be reckoned with on the Internet—for the rest of the decade.

HEARD IN THE '90s

"Sometimes the only sane answer to an insane world is insanity."
—Fox Mulder, *The X-Files*

"It had heart. . . . The lead characters, you were sympathetic with. They were dealing with issues you could relate to—if your life was really freaky."
—Penelope Spheeris, director

REASON #58 1999

Y2K Scare

People called it Armageddon, Doomsday, the end of the world. All anyone could talk about in 1999 was what was to going to happen in 2000. Would computer chips be able to comprehend the 2000 digits? Would they be able to figure out what day it was, or would they crash and burn, leaving us to fend for ourselves? On the night before the world was going to end, America hunkered down and stocked up—on water, cash, batteries. We braced ourselves for the worst. Except the worst never came. The ball dropped, it was January 1 of the new millennium, and everything still worked: ATM machines, our TV sets, laptops, and DVD players. It turned out computers weren't as dumb as . . . we were.

"I was like really excited about it actually. Everyone was like 'everything's going to shut down, it's going to be chaos.' . . . I was all excited about it, and then nothing happened. Yeah, thanks . . ."

—Nicole Richie

REASON #57 1995

Clueless

A my Heckerling (*Fast Times at Ridgemont High*) directed and Alicia Silverstone starred in this homage to Jane Austen's classic novel *Emma.* Cher Horowitz (Silverstone) is a wealthy Beverly Hills High School student who channels her considerable energy into making over a "clueless" new kid named Tai (played by Brittany Murphy). But Cher's grand gesture backfires when Tai becomes interested in Cher's stepbrother, Josh, stirring up surprising feelings. Cher's got some serious soul-searching to do, which she does while sporting super cute designer duds. *Clueless* grossed more than 75 million dollars, introduced phrases like "As if!" into the national lexicon, and made Silverstone a superstar. In 1996, it spawned a TV series, but Silverstone did not return. Cher was instead played by Rachel Blanchard, who would later play another fashion-obsessed teen in the movie *Mean Girls.*

REASON #56 1997

Hanson

The trio of brothers from Tulsa, Oklahoma, was the decade's answer to the Beach Boys or the Jackson Five. Their first single, "MMMBop," was the guilty pleasure hit of the year, selling 8 million copies worldwide and turning the blond photogenic brothers, Isaac, Taylor, and Zac, into media celebrities. The song also helped garner three 1998 Grammy nominations for the band, including Record of the Year, Best New Artist, and Best Pop Performance by a Duo or Group.

"Oh, so hold on to the ones who really care. In the end they'll be the only ones there. When you get old and start losing your hair, can you tell me who will still care? Can you tell me who will still care? Oh care. MMMBop, ba duba dop ba do bop, ba duba dop ba do bop, ba duba dop ba do . . ."

—Hanson, "MMMBop"

REASON #55 1999

Who Wants to Be a Millionaire

A remake of a British quiz show *Who Wants to Be a Millionaire* invigorated the ABC network and broadened the career of Regis Philbin, the veteran entertainer and longtime host of *Live with Regis and Kathie Lee*. The trivia game show was a surprise hit and quickly became a phenomenon. ABC couldn't broadcast the show often enough. They bumped it from once to twice a week, then to four!

Prime time breathed new life into Regis. His trademark "Is that your final answer?" became an American catchphrase; his monochromatic duds—dark shirt and dark tie, usually shiny—started a fashion trend in men's clothing. There were *Millionaire* books, board games, and CD-ROMs. There were celebrity *Millionaire* editions. And of course there were copycats, like Fox's *Greed* and NBC's *Weakest Link*. Finally, *Millionaire* mania eased and Regis returned to daytime. The show eventually reemerged in a syndicated incarnation hosted by another veteran talker, *The View*'s Meredith Vieira.

REASON #54 1995

The WB

The face of this fledgling network was a green cartoon frog. Michigan J. Frog—*yes, he actually had a name*—didn't last. The WB did—despite the fact that in its banner year the network hedged its bets on teen-helmed sitcoms like *Kirk*, starring Kirk Cameron, and *Brotherly Love*, starring Joey "Whoa" Lawrence. But sitcoms weren't what young audiences were after, and the WB didn't strike it big until launching teen-populated hourlong dramas. *7th Heaven* and *Buffy the Vampire Slayer* were the first big hits. Next came *Dawson's Creek, Felicity*, and the Buffy spin-off *Angel*. Good-bye, Frog. Hello, marketable stars Sarah Michelle Gellar, Keri Russell, and Katie Holmes . . .

HEARD IN THE '90s

"This is the '90s. You don't just go around punching people. You have to say something cool first."
—Joe Hallenback,
The Last Boy Scout, 1991

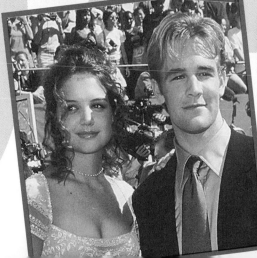

REASON #53 | 1996

Swingers

Vince Vaughn and Jon Favreau starred in this low-budget hit (which Favreau also wrote), an ode to Los Angeles nightlife that capitalized on the decade's retro-fascination with hep cats, the Rat Pack, lounge culture, and swing dancing. Guys referred to girls as "babies," and "You're so money," was the compliment of choice. Even today, if you hear someone say, "Vegas, baby, Vegas!" they're probably quoting *Swingers*. Aside from making Vince Vaughn a national sensation, the free-spirited flick also featured a then-little-known actress by the name of Heather Graham.

"Look, we're gonna spend half the night driving around the Hills looking for this one party and you're going to say it sucks and we're all gonna leave and then we're gonna go look for this other party. But all the parties and all the bars, they all suck. I spend half the night talking to some girl who's looking around the room to see if there's somebody else who's more important she should be talking to. And it's like I'm supposed to be all happy 'cause she's wearing a backpack, you know?"

—Mike (Jon Favreau), *Swingers*

REASON #52 1992

Men Are from Mars, Women Are from Venus

M en and women are inherently different, or so proclaimed relationship guru John Gray, the mastermind behind the decade's biggest self-help book. Fourteen million people paid good money to read about Gray's interplanetary philosophy—despite the fact that the guy got his Ph.D. via correspondence courses and was once a celibate monk. People lapped up Gray's astrological love advice, and he kept it coming, sequel after sequel, including the aptly titled *Mars and Venus on a Date* and *Mars and Venus in the Bedroom.*

Bestselling Self-Help
Books of the '90s

If Life Is a Game, These Are the Rules
by Cherie Carter-Scott

Something More: Excavating Your Authentic Self
by Sarah Ban Breathnach

*The Dilbert Principle: A Cubicle's-Eye View of Bosses,
Meetings, Management Fads and Other Workplace Afflictions*
by Scott Adams

*A Return to Love: Reflections on the Principles of "A Course in
Miracles"*
by Marianne Williamson

*Financial Self-Defense: How to Win the Fight for Financial
Freedom*
by Charles J. Givens

Homecoming: Reclaiming and Championing Your Inner Child
by John Bradshaw

*Wealth Without Risk: How to Develop a Personal Fortune
Without Going Out on a Limb*
by Charles J. Givens

REASON #51 1997

Austin Powers: International Man of Mystery

The outrageous, psychedelic creation of *Saturday Night Live* alum Mike Meyers, Austin Powers was an international man of mystery, a cryogenically frozen '60s super sleuth who was defrosted in present day to save the world from the diabolical (and bald) Dr. Evil. Tell us, baby, does he make you horny?

"Shall we shag now, or shall we shag later? How do you like to do it? Do you like to wash up first?"
—Austin Powers

REASON #50 | 1996

The Rosie O'Donnell Show

THE STATS

- *The Rosie O'Donnell Show* debuted on June 10, 1996.

- The first guest was *ER*'s **George Clooney.**

- The second guest was *All My Children*'s Susan Lucci.

- It was the **highest-rated premiere** of any daytime talk show in the '90s.

- It was estimated that O'Donnell shot more than 15,000 **Koosh balls** into the audience in her first year on the air.

- In 1997, O'Donnell published *Kids Are Punny: Jokes Sent by Kids to "The Rosie O'Donnell Show."* All proceeds went to O'Donnell's charity.

- Rosie spent much of the first year gushing about what a **cutie patootie** Tom Cruise was. He made his first appearance on her show in December 1996.

The Late-Night Wars

When late-night talk show host Johnny Carson bid adieu to television, a war erupted between his two possible *Tonight Show* successors. David Letterman, the host of *Late Night with David Letterman*, which aired after *The Tonight Show*, duked it out with Jay Leno, Carson's frequent *Tonight Show* guest host, for the coveted time slot. When Leno won, Dave ditched, jumping ship for a rival time slot at CBS. The heavyweight bout was chronicled in the bestselling book, *The Late Shift*, which was later made into an award-winning movie on HBO.

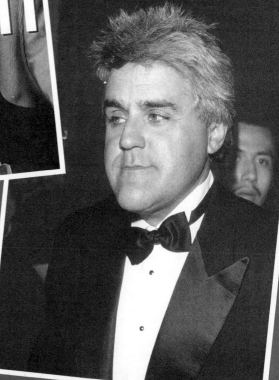

Evita

It was a hit Broadway musical in the '80s and a lavish musical motion picture in the '90s. *Evita* was the story of Evita Perón, née Evita Duarte, who marries politician Juan Perón, the eventual president of Argentina. While the Argentinean elite shun Evita, the country's less fortunate make her a hero. Sadly, she dies an early tragic death without achieving political success on her own merits. In the movie directed by Alan Parker, Madonna plays Evita and Antonio Banderas—the object of her affection in her documentary *Madonna: Truth or Dare*—plays Ché. The movie left many critics pondering the question, "Who knew Madonna could actually *sing?*"

OTHER ACTRESSES SUPPOSEDLY UP FOR THE PART OF EVITA

Meryl Streep

Michelle Pfeiffer

Barbra Streisand

Liza Minnelli

REASON #47 1990

M. C. Hammer

P*lease Hammer Don't Hurt 'Em!* was the name of the album; "U Can't Touch This" was the debut single. The catchy hit was built around a sample from Rick James's classic *Super Freak,* and it made rapper and dancer M. C. Hammer, born Stanley Kirk Burrell, a star. In his trademark balloon pants—dubbed *Hammer* Pants— M. C. Hammer was an MTV mainstay of the early '90s. In 1994, Hammer tried on a harder "gangsta" edge, and disillusioned many fans. Then he went bankrupt due to over-spending. By the end of the '90s, Hammer had regained his footing, and he found a place for himself at the pulpit when he became a preacher.

"M. C. Hammer was hot, don't even twist it!"

—Lil' Bow Wow

REASON #46 1994

Hugh Grant

H e was shaggy-haired, he stammered, and he was oh so cute. His breakout hit was *Four Weddings and a Funeral,* the ensemble hit about English chums, directed by Mike Newell. Andie MacDowell also starred as the object of Grant's character's adoration—he admitted his love by quoting David Cassidy from *The Partridge Family:* "I think I love you," he charmingly stuttered. Gray, gloomy England never looked so good, and socially inept, skinny, pale guys never looked so dashing!

Despite one highly publicized misstep, Hugh Grant stayed true—at least publicly—to one woman in the '90s. Elizabeth Hurley followed Grant into the limelight, then snagged it for herself. Her most memorable moment? Wearing an iconic outfit that became commonly known as "the safety pin dress."

REASON #45 1990

In Living Color

THE STATS

- *In Living Color* aired on Fox from 1990 to 1994.

- The sketch comedy show was the brainchild of Keenen Ivory Wayans, the second-eldest Wayans sibling. Kim, Damon, Marlon, and Shawn Wayans were also on the show.

- Non-Wayans included Jamie Foxx, Jim Carrey, Tommy Davidson, and Kim Coles.

- Popular sketches were "Homey D. Clown," "Men on Film," "Ugly Wanda," and "Fire Marshal Bill."

- The series featured a troupe of hip-hop dancers called "Fly Girls" who opened and closed the show. One of them was . . . Jennifer Lopez.

REASON #44

JFK Jr.

John F. Kennedy Junior began the decade working for the Manhattan District Attorney's Office. When he resigned to pursue other ventures, many speculated that it would be politics. Instead, it was publishing. In 1995, Kennedy debuted *George,* a glossy monthly magazine with the slogan: Not just politics as usual. Kennedy edited and wrote for the magazine, even contributing interviews with Fidel Castro and Mike Tyson. Famous for being one of the country's most eligible bachelors, Kennedy ended his single days in 1996, when he married Calvin Klein publicist Carolyn Bessette. They died in a plane crash off the coast of Martha's Vineyard in 1999.

"He was everywhere. He seemed like a man of the people even though he lived in an ivory tower. To me, he was somebody who could accomplish whatever he wanted and maybe might be a future president."

—Michael Musto

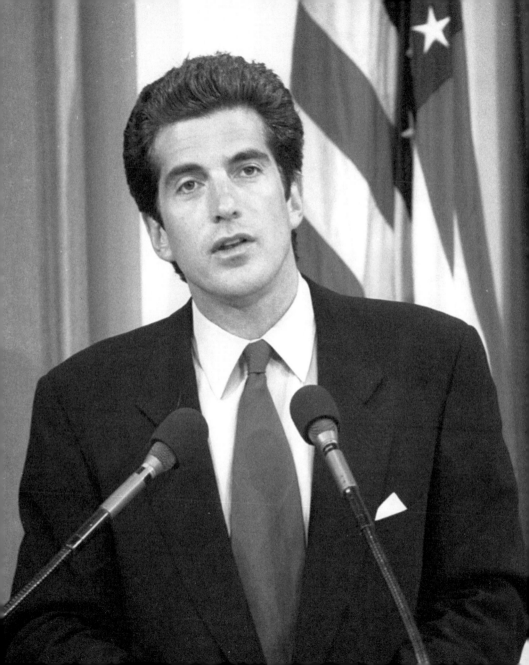

REASON #43 1991 and 1996

Lollapalooza & Lilith Fair

Jane's Addiction front man Perry Farrell organized this twenty-city musical extravaganza originally envisioned as Jane's Addiction's farewell tour. The festival was a traveling counter-culture carnival that offered daylong concerts of alternative music (Hole, Smashing Pumpkins, Beastie Boys), tattoo artists, trippy virtual reality tents, and lots o' moshing.

In 1997, Sarah McLachlan got in on the action with Lilith Fair, an all-female music festival that matched musicians like Jewel, Paula Cole, and Tracy Chapman with New Age boutiques and political organizations. One ticket bought you the opportunity to hear Liz Phair perform, get your arm henna-tattooed, and register to vote. Talk about multitasking!

ALSO IN 1996...

McDonald's launches a massive advertising campaign for the Arch Deluxe.

REASON #42

Grunge

FASHION OF THE '90s
THE STAPLES

- Ripped jeans
- Combat boots
- Plaid flannel shirts
- Birkenstocks
- Unraveling sweaters
- Bed head
- Vintage housedresses
- Long-underwear tops
- Scraggly facial hair
- Hygiene optional

"I think grunge was an important thing in the '90s . . . It made a huge impact."

—Cynthia Rowley

REASON #41

Baywatch

There was no bigger syndicated success in the '90s than the long-running TV series *Baywatch,* a soapy drama about hot Los Angeles County lifeguards on a beach that made stars of Pamela Anderson, Traci Bingham, Michael Bergin, and Yasmine Bleeth. David Hasselhoff played Mitch Buchannon, the wizened lifeguard charged to protect his ensemble of bathing beauties, who patrolled the beach in skimpy red bathing suits. Raging seas and hormones kept this show afloat for the entire decade. Has mouth-to-mouth resuscitation ever looked so appealing?

REASON #40 | 1993

Stop the Insanity!

S usan Powter was the tyrannical diet guru whose pro-exercise, anti-fad diet tirades made her a household name in the mid-'90s. Infor-mercials, books, and workout videos featured the spiky-haired blonde's energetic, in-your-face attitude. Powter herself once had a weight problem, and the fact that she'd kept the pounds off made believers out of dieters across the country. Her books were *New York Times* bestsellers, and she even had her own daytime talk show for a spell.

Remember These?

DIET FADS OF THE '90s

Richard Simmons

Suzanne Somers

Dr. Barry Sears (The Zone)

Sugar Busters!

The Cabbage Soup Diet

Slim-Fast

Phen-Fen

Stop the Insanity!

Eat • Breathe • Move

Change the way you look and feel – forever

SUSAN POWTER

Starbucks

A modest Seattle storefront sparked a coffee revolution when the Northwest startup went national. Suddenly, coffee drinkers had a new vocabulary: *venti, grande, extra foam, macchiato, Frappuccino.* Competitors scrambled to keep up. They couldn't. Starbucks was the retail sensation of the '90s. By the end of the decade, there were five thousand Starbucks across the country—that means ten new stores were launched per week. Odds are good that a new Starbucks outpost opened somewhere in America just while you were reading this entry.

"Something happened to us in the '90s. All of a sudden, we were okay with paying $4.00 for coffee and water."
—Tina Malave, entertainment reporter

REASON #38 1997

Matt and Ben

They were childhood buddies, writers and actors both, and in 1997, a script they cowrote was nominated for nine Oscars and won for Best Original Screenplay. They also costarred in the film. It was *Good Will Hunting,* their names were Matt Damon and Ben Affleck, and we haven't stopped talking about them since. *Good Will Hunting* was a launching pad for Matt and Ben. In the two years that followed, Affleck did a turn as an action star in *Armageddon,* directed by Michael Bay; and then appeared in the Academy Award–winning *Shakespeare in Love.* Damon starred in Steven Spielberg's World War II pic *Saving Private Ryan* as well as *The Talented Mr. Ripley.* Both appeared in 1999's *Dogma,* directed by their old friend Kevin Smith, of *Clerks* and *Chasing Amy* fame. If it wasn't Matt's and Ben's movies that were snaring headlines, it was their star-crossed love lives: In the late '90's Damon dated Minnie Driver and Winona Ryder; Affleck got involved with Gwyneth Paltrow. None of the relationships lasted.

ALSO IN 1997 . . .

Dolly the sheep becomes the first mammal to be cloned.

HEARD IN THE '90s

Dr. Ian Malcolm: God creates dinosaurs. God destroys dinosaurs. God creates man. Man destroys God. Man creates dinosaurs . . .

Dr. Ellie Sattler: Dinosaurs eat man. Woman inherits the earth. . . .

—*Jurassic Park,* 1993

REASON #37 | 1993

Jurassic Park

Who knew velociraptors were "small active carnivores that probably fed on protocer- atops; possibly related more closely to birds than to other dinosaurs?" Before 1993, hardly anyone. But after Steven Spielberg's *Jurassic Park* hit the big screen, dinosaurs made a major comeback, and all of America knew the difference between a raptor and a baby triceratops. The dino-flick, based on Michael Crichton's bestselling book, boasted a stellar cast—including Sam Neill, Jeff Goldblum, and Laura Dern—and a meaty plot: Scientists use DNA to clone dinosaurs for a megalomaniac's dream dinosaur theme park. Mayhem erupts when a techie disables the security system as part of a plot to steal dino-embryos, and the dinosaurs escape.

The film raked in close to a billion dollars worldwide at the box office, thanks to mes- merizing special effects that involved the use of actual dinosaur-size animatrons. *Jurassic Park* was also a merchandising bonanza; its storyline about a theme park allowed for inno- vative product placement—many of the items featured in the film were prototypes for ac- tual retail products for sale. *Jurassic Park* held the title as the decade's most successful film until *Titanic* toppled it in 1997. But don't feel too bad. By the decade's end, *Jurassic Park* had spawned an amusement park attraction, an animated series, and a sequel.

REASON #36

Garth Brooks

He was a barrier-breaking crooner who did the inconceivable: He brought country music into the mainstream. In 1990, Garth Brooks's album *No Fences,* buoyed by the hit single "Friends in Low Places," rose to the top of the country charts. It did phenomenal numbers for a country album—for any album, actually—selling 700,000 copies in the first ten days of release. Brooks promoted the album by performing sold-out arena-style tours that resembled Rolling Stones concerts more than traditional country shows. The success of *No Fences* set the stage for Garth's follow-up album, *Ropin' the Wind* which became the first country album ever to debut at the top of the pop charts.

> "If God came down here with the box that had the reason for living in it, I'd like to find just two words: The Music. That would be neat."
> —Garth Brooks

REASON #35

The Hip-Hop Influence

"Hat 2 da back I gotta kick my pants down real low. That's the kinda girl I am."

—TLC, *"Hat 2 Da Back,"* from *Oooooooohhh . . . On the TLC Tip*

IMPORTANT MOMENTS IN '90s HIP-HOP FASHION

- Russell Simmons launches Phat Farm in 1992.

- Timberland boots gain hip-hop credibility.

- Tommy Hilfiger becomes a designer of choice for preppy/baggy clothes.

- The Air Jordan is the most popular selling sneaker of the decade.

- The Beastie Boys invest in the clothing company X Large.

- Sean "Puffy" Combs launches his own design label, Sean John, in 1998.

121

REASON #34 1992

Absolutely Fabulous

Sweetie, darling, sweetie, darling . . . It was all anyone could say when in 1992 Comedy Central began running British import *Absolutely Fabulous,* a half-hour comedy about two boozy fashionistas living in posh London. Jennifer Saunders played the self-obsessed Edina; Joanna Lumley was sexaholic Patsy; Julia Sawalha was Saffron, Edina's frumpy daughter. It was one misadventure after the next as Edina and Patsy experimented with colonic irrigation, liposuction, isolation tanks, and endless amounts of pills and alcohol.

"Patsy has sex like a man. She has boys, picks them up, it means nothing to her. . . . She can drink you under the table. She knows swear words I've never heard, and she can fall over really brilliantly—a rare talent!"

—Jennifer Saunders

HEARD IN THE '90s

Edina: What you two don't seem to realize is that inside of me, there is a thin person just screaming to get out.

Gran: Just the one, dear?

—*Absolutely Fabulous*

REASON #33 1992

Baby Got Back

S ir Mix-a-Lot's rump-tastic anthem to big booty sold more than 2 million copies, and spent five weeks on top of the pop charts. He may have been a one-hit wonder, but with that one hit, Sir Mix-a-Lot boosted the body image of women everywhere.

"So your girlfriend rolls a Honda, playin' workout tapes by Fonda. But Fonda ain't got a motor in the back of her Honda."
—Sir Mix-a-Lot, "Baby Got Back"

HEARD IN THE '90s

"It's the '90s. Plastic surgery is like good grooming."
—Elise, *The First Wives Club*

SPOTLIGHT ON ...
CRYSTAL PEPSI—1992

It tasted like Pepsi, but it looked like water, hence being marketed as the "Clear Alternative." In 1992, Pepsi launched a massive ad campaign using Van Halen's anthem, "Right Now." Except soda drinkers said, "Not now," and Crystal Pepsi was whisked off shelves. That didn't stop the Coca-Cola Company from going the colorless route. Soon after, they introduced Tab Clear.

ALSO IN 1992 ...

Marisa Tomei wins a Best Supporting Actress Oscar or her role in *My Cousin Vinny.*

REASON #32 1994

Nancy Kerrigan vs. Tonya Harding

J anuary 1994: U.S. figure skater and Olympic hopeful Nancy Kerrigan had just completed a practice session for the U.S. World Championships when she was brutally clubbed in the leg by an assailant. It was called "the whack heard 'round the world," and the investigation led to a shocking revelation: There'd been a plot to take Kerrigan down, and another skater was being implicated. She was Tonya Harding, and her ex-husband's friend turned out to be Kerrigan's assailant. Harding claimed no prior knowledge of the incident, but later pleaded guilty to hindering the investigation.

Harding was allowed to participate in the Olympic Games despite the ongoing investigation. After a lot of hoopla and some *verrrry* tense group practices, the Winter Olympics passed without random acts of violence. Kerrigan won the silver; Harding finished eighth.

"I was on Tonya Harding's side. . . . I love my little white trash princess with the crispy bangs."
—Kathy Griffin

REASON #31 1990

Ghost

The tag line was: "You will believe." And whether you did or didn't, you still probably went to see *Ghost,* the Patrick Swayze–Demi Moore–Whoopi Goldberg vehicle that won Goldberg an Academy Award. Moore and Swayze played Molly and Sam, a New York City couple in love. While walking home one night from a date, they're accosted by a thief and Sam is murdered. Oddly, Sam's spirit remains on earth—and there's only one person who can communicate with him: Whoopi Goldberg's character Oda Mae Brown, a con artist posing as a psychic. Sam realizes his death was not an accident, and he has to warn Molly that she's in danger too. Oda Mae to the rescue! (Also . . . the movie managed to make pottery sexy. Now, that's an impressive achievement!)

"*Ghost* forever linked two things in the American consciousness that can never come apart: 'Unchained Melody' and pottery."

—Teresa Strasser, journalist

REASON #30 1992

Ross Perot

He was a Texas tycoon with lots of sass and loads more cash, and in 1992, he ran for president on the Independent ticket. H. Ross Perot preached a plan for responsible government—"Get rid of all the perks," he said with regard to free parking for government officials. His campaign cost $57 million, which seemed to be for naught when he dropped out of the race in July. But he reentered it in October, splitting the Republican vote, and helping Bill Clinton claim victory. In 1996, he was back as the candidate for the Reform Party, a political party he founded.

America may not have wanted Perot to be president, but we sure found his eccentric personality entertaining—and were even more entertained by Dana Carvey's dead-on impersonation of the wily tycoon on *Saturday Night Live.*

"If you see a snake, just kill it—don't appoint a committee on snakes."

—H. Ross Perot

Other '90s Milestones

1990   There's a new feature film
           rating: NC-17.

1991   Advertisements for condoms
           appear on television.

1995   Lettuce is sold in a bag.

1996   Prince Charles and Princess
           Diana get divorced.

1998   Europe gets its own official
           currency, the Euro.

1998   The 5,000th episode of game
           show *The Price Is Right* airs
           on CBS.

1999   The second Woodstock
           festival takes place.

REASON #29 1999

HBO

I n 1999, for the very first time in television history, a cable channel was nominated for more Emmy Awards than any of the broadcast networks. HBO's haul included wins for best writing and directing in a miniseries (*The Corner*) and best lead actress (Edie Falco in *The Sopranos.*)

"They pushed a lot of boundaries. You saw a lot of things on *Sex and the City* that you could never see on network television. It was a sign of the times. In the late nineties, people were ready for that."

—Kristin Veitch

REASON #28

Tom Hanks

From 1992 to 1995, actor Tom Hanks was on a winning streak, starring in six top-grossing movies. His streak began with Penny Marshall's *A League of Their Own.* Hanks played crotchety has-been Jimmy Dugan, who's stuck coaching an all-women's baseball team. ("There's no crying in baseball!" became his signature line.) He went from grouchy malcontent to stoic single parent, and object of female adoration, when Nora Ephron gave him the lead in the swoony romantic picture *Sleepless in Seattle.* In 1993 came Jonathan Demme's *Philadelphia.* Hanks's performance as a gay man dying of AIDS won him an Oscar for Best Actor in a Leading Role. In 1994, he made history when he repeated the feat, winning for his performance in *Forrest Gump.* He was the first actor to win back-to-back leading-man Oscars since Spencer Tracy in the 1930s. *Apollo 13,* in 1995, earned Hanks yet another Oscar nomination, but he didn't win. In 1996, Hanks even got behind the camera to direct *That Thing You Do!* a film about a '60s pop band grappling with instant fame. On-screen, Hanks played the band's greedy manager.

In his acceptance speech for *Philadelphia,* Hanks gave a shout-out to his gay high school drama coach, which inspired the Kevin Kline comedy *In & Out,* about what happens to a small-town teacher when a former student turned star actor outs him at the Academy Awards.

"Look, I'm the luckiest man in the world. I have a lot of stuff I have to deal with, and some-times that gets the best of you, but by and large the best good fortune I have is that I get to do something for a living that gives me great pleasure."
—Tom Hanks

REASON #27

Tupac Shakur

1971–1996

The Notorious B.I.G.

1972–1997

"Reality is wrong.
Dreams are for
real."
—Tupac Shakur

"Learn to treat life to
the best, put stress to
rest. . . ."
—The Notorious B.I.G.

REASON #26

Wayne's World

THE STATS

- In 1992, the popular *Saturday Night Live* sketch about two dudes from Aurora, Illinois, who broadcast a public-access show from their basement became a feature-length film starring Mike Myers and Dana Carvey.

- The tag line for the first movie was: "You'll laugh. You'll cry. You'll hurl." The tag line for the 1993 sequel *Wayne's World 2* was "You'll laugh. You'll cry. You'll hurl again."

- *Wayne's World* popularized its own brand of slacker speak, and can be wholly blamed for the popularity of the following phrases: "Not!," "Party on, dude!," "babelicious," "shwing!," "We're not worthy!," "Ex-squeeze me?," "No way! . . . Way!," and "Yeah, and monkeys might fly outta my butt!"

"I once thought I had mono for an entire year. It turned out I was just really bored."

—*Wayne's World*

REASON #25 | 1994

My So-Called Life

From the producers of *thirtysomething* came this extraordinary drama about an ordinary girl. Angela Chase was fifteen, full of questions, full of life, and just a little full of herself. In the pilot episode, she dyed her hair red, ditched her best friend, made two new ones, obsessed about a crush, and sniped at her parents. Claire Danes played Angela—she was only thirteen at the time. Rarely has a television show so critically acclaimed been given so small a chance. ABC aired nineteen episodes of *My So-Called Life,* before pulling it off the air due to low ratings. It's lived on as a fondly remembered cult classic ever since.

"The only reason I watched *My So-Called Life* was to see Jared Leto, because he's so hot. And he never said anything! He just sat there and was depressed the whole time. I was like: 'Ahhhh, love you!'"

—Nicole Richie

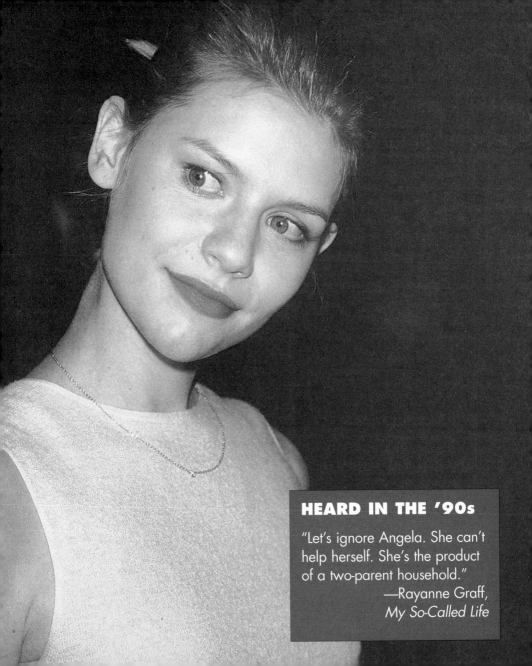

HEARD IN THE '90s

"Let's ignore Angela. She can't help herself. She's the product of a two-parent household."

—Rayanne Graff,
My So-Called Life

REASON #24

Jim Carrey

1990	*In Living Color*
1994	*Ace Ventura: Pet Detective*
1994	*The Mask*
1994	*Dumb and Dumber*
1995	*Batman Forever*
1995	*Ace Ventura: When Nature Calls*
1996	*The Cable Guy*
1997	*Liar Liar*
1998	*The Truman Show*
1999	*Man on the Moon*

REASON #23 1997

Backstreet Boys

I f the names Kevin, Brian, Howie, A.J., and Nick mean nothing to you, then you definitely weren't a teenager in the mid-'90s. They were The Backstreet Boys, who pioneered the boy-band genre and the sappy pop sound that dominated popular radio in the late '90s. With hits like "Quit Playing Games (With My Heart)," "As Long as You Love Me," "I Want It That Way," the five-man group paved the way for other boy-band wonders like 'N SYNC and 98°.

ALSO IN 1997...

Emeril Live premieres on the Food Network.

REASON #22 1996

Tiger Woods

Golf was a sport dominated by older white men until 1996, when Tiger Woods, a half black, half Thai twenty-year-old wunderkind, turned pro. In 1997, Tiger became both the first golfer with a multiracial background and the youngest competitor to win the Masters. In 1999, Woods won his second major competition, the PGA Championship. Seeing a young man of color leading the world of golf inspired economically disadvantaged young people to follow the sport, and many even took up playing. Tiger dominated the golf scene for the rest of the decade, eventually becoming the first golfer to hold all four major professional titles at the same time.

"I'm a golf junkie. I'm hooked really badly. It's, like, the best metaphor for life that there is in sports. Through those 18 holes, you're up, you're down. You hit a bad shot, you're out. But your next shot is incredible, and you're back in it again. You can play golf with someone and tell what kind of person they are without ever hearing them talk."

—Will Smith

REASON #21 | 1991

The Jerry Springer Show

"**M**y Wife Weighs 900 Pounds!" "Woman in Labor Confronts Mistress!" "Surprise, I'm a Transsexual!" Doesn't that just say it all? In 1991, America welcomed into its home this over-the-top syndicated daytime talk show hosted by a former Cincinnati mayor. What do you get when you cross brawls and catfights with bitches, pimps, and hos? A genre-defining hit.

"The Jerry Springer Show took the country by storm, thus insuring that any intelligent alien life who might be monitoring our planet would skip our trailer park trash galaxy."

—Vance DeGeneres

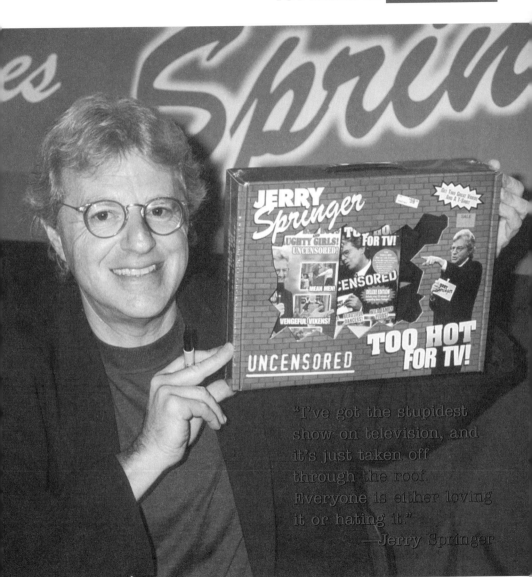

"I've got the stupidest show on television, and it's just taken off through the roof. Everyone is either loving it or hating it."

—Jerry Springer

REASON #20 1993

NYPD Blue

I t came with a warning: "This police drama contains adult language and scenes with partial nudity. Viewer discretion is advised." It was touted as the first R-rated TV show on network television. *NYPD Blue,* Steven Bochco's gritty prime-time police drama, has seen detectives come and go, but since *Blue*'s debut in 1993 the show has held on to viewers. The first season starred Dennis Franz and David Caruso as Sipowicz and Kelly, emotionally complex members of the Fifteenth Precinct's detective unit. It turned out that Caruso was as complicated as his fictional alter ego—he shocked viewers and coworkers by ditching the series four shows into its second season. Critics wondered if the show would last without him. It did. Jimmy Smits joined as Bobby Simone and brought increased ratings with him. Other stars who came and went were Kim Delaney, Rick Schroder, and Mark-Paul Gosselaar of *Saved by the Bell* fame. Four-time Emmy Award winner Dennis Franz wisely stayed put.

"In spite of those who seek to legislate what we can and cannot see on our own television sets in the privacy of our own homes, *NYPD Blue* has succeeded because the American people, properly so, prefer to judge for themselves."

—Steven Bochco at
The People's Choice Awards

REASON #19

Diana

I n the summer of 1981, the must-see television event of the summer was the wedding of England's Prince Charles to Lady Diana Spencer. He was thirty-two. She was twenty. The next years were bountiful for the young princess. She fulfilled her royal duty by producing two male heirs to the throne, Prince William and Prince Harry; she struggled with the trials of public life; she became a champion of charitable causes; and somewhere along the way she had the time to become a world-renowned style icon, as well as the most beloved royal in the world. But for Diana, that love came with a price, and in the summer of 1997, the world mourned her untimely death in an accident that occurred while her car was pursued by paparazzi.

Though she was divorced from Charles and no longer an official member of the House of Windsor, Diana received a funeral befitting "the people's princess," and 2.5 billion television viewers watched as a four-mile procession brought her coffin from Kensington Palace to Westminster Abbey, where a service attended by politicians, family members, and celebrities honored her. Her brother Earl Spencer eulogized her, and her friend Elton John performed his newly reworked song "Candle in the Wind." A private burial followed at the Spencer family's estate at Althorp.

> "Of all the ironies about Diana, perhaps the greatest is this: that a girl given the name of the ancient goddess of hunting was, in the end, the most hunted person in the modern age."
>
> —Earl Spencer

REASON #18 1994

Reality Bites

Winona Ryder, Ethan Hawke, Janeane Garofalo, and Ben Stiller star in this Gen-X classic about college grads making their way—or *not*—in the world. Winona Ryder plays Lelaina, an aspiring filmmaker toiling as a production assistant on a cheesy morning show. When Lelaina crashes into cable exec Michael (Ben Stiller)'s car, they embark on a personal and business relationship. But Lelaina's not ready for the yuppie values Michael personifies. And when he turns her home movies into a *Real World*–style reality show, she can't ditch him fast enough, heading straight into the arms of Troy—Ethan Hawke—with a chinful of facial hair. Self-obsessed drama and copious pop-culture references ensue. . . .

ALSO IN 1997 . . .

For the first time, students are allowed to bring calculators to the SAT exams.

REASON #17

Brad Pitt

1991	*Thelma & Louise*
1991	*Johnny Suede*
1992	*Cool World*
1992	*A River Runs Through It*
1993	*Kalifornia*
1993	*True Romance*
1994	*The Favor*
1994	*Interview with the Vampire: The Vampire Chronicles*
1995	*Se7en*
1995	*Twelve Monkeys*
1996	*Sleepers*
1997	*The Devil's Own*
1997	*Seven Years in Tibet*
1997	*The Dark Side of the Sun*
1998	*Meet Joe Black*
1999	*Fight Club*

REASON #16 1994

O. J. Simpson

I f there's a generation of Americans who can answer the questions, "Where were you when JFK was shot?", there's another who are able to say exactly where they were during the O.J. Simpson car chase. On June 12th, 1994, football legend O.J. "The Juice" Simpson's ex-wife, Nicole Brown Simpson, and her friend Ronald Goldman were brutally murdered at her Brentwood home. Evidence suggested O.J. was the prime suspect; and the day after the funeral, the police sought his arrest. O.J. was supposed to turn himself in on the morning of June 17. Instead, he took to the road. Armed with cash, his passport, a disguise, and a loaded gun, O.J. and his buddy, ex-teammate Al Cowlings, got on the San Diego Freeway (I5-S) driving a white Ford Bronco. Soon police were hot on their trail, and what followed was the most exciting low-speed chase in criminal justice history. That evening, Simpson returned to his Brentwood home and finally surrendered. The criminal trial that followed was broadcast on daytime TV and introduced the nation to a host of characters: the somber Judge Lance Ito; the beleaguered prosecutors Chris Darden and Marcia Clark; the flamboyant defense team, most notably Johnnie Cochran and Robert Shapiro; and witnesses Kato Kaelin and Detective Mark Fuhrman. The saga—at least this chapter of it—ended on October 3, 1995, when after only five hours' deliberation the jury found Simpson not guilty on all counts.

REASON #15

No Paris Hilton.

REASON #14

Tom Cruise and Nicole Kidman

The decade's most high-powered and highly visible Hollywood couple were married for the entire decade, with tabloids—and fans—following their every move. The two broke up in a very public divorce in 2001.

REASON #13 1992

The Real World

I f, in 1992, critics thought MTV's *The Real World* was creepily voyeuristic, what must they think of television now? *The Real World* placed seven strangers (and a mess of cameras) in a fabulously decorated apartment and found out what happened when people stop being polite and start getting real. . . . The premiere season of America's first reality show seems tame, classy, even subdued compared to the bug-eating, wife-swapping series on television in the new millennium. Eric, Julie, Norm, Becky, Andre, Kevin, and Heather B. moved into a Manhattan loft and mulled over their futures while engaging in daily squabbles. It seems unbelievable that Julie and Kevin's sidewalk fight about whether people of color could be racist could have commanded water-cooler chatter, but in those days it all seemed so new.

ALSO IN 1992 . . .

Innovative rap group Arrested Development wins the Grammy Award for Best New Artist.

REASON #12

SNL

I n 1990, late-night sketch show *Saturday Night Live* had been on the air for fifteen years, but it hadn't lived up to its heady glory days of the late '70s, the bygone era of John Belushi and Dan Aykroyd, Chevy Chase, and Gilda Radner. But *Saturday Night Live* was about to get a really good anniversary present: a Second Coming. Cast members for the 1990–1991 season included Dana Carvey, Phil Hartman, and Mike Myers. Chris Farley, Chris Rock, Adam Sandler, Rob Schneider, David Spade, and Julia Sweeney were featured performers. Phil Hartman provided the Bill Clinton impersonations; Dana Carvey did George Bush (Senior) and Ross Perot. A new roster of classic sketches was born: "Wayne's World," Carvey's "The Church Lady," Hartman's "Unfrozen Caveman Lawyer," Adam Sandler's "Opera Man," Mike Myer's "Coffee Talk with Linda Richman," and Julia Sweeney's androgynous "Pat."

REASON #11 1999

The Blair Witch Project

In 1999, *The Blair Witch Project* debuted at the Sundance Film Festival. It was one of the many small, gritty low-budgets debuting that year, but there was something special about this one. Early Internet buzz had people wondering about the intriguing plot, involving three student filmmakers who try to document a Maryland local legend called the Blair Witch. Was there really a Blair Witch? Was this film based on a true story? Was it the actual lost footage of the poor intrepid students? Viewers desperate for clues lined up for the film's midnight screening. Buyers, too. And before the sun had risen, Artisan purchased the movie for a whopping 1.1 million dollars—this despite the fact that the mock-documentary by three Central Florida film students, featured a cast of total unknowns, and cost only about $35,000 to make. Rest assured, it was a wise investment. By year's end, *The Blair Witch Project* grossed more than 240 million dollars worldwide, making it the biggest independent movie of its time. Its hand-held camcorder style made it easy to imitate, and in the wake of the film's success there were loads of imitators as well as spoofs like *The Blair Bitch Project,* starring *Exorcist* actress Linda Blair, and *The Tony Blair Witch Project.*

"I am so, so sorry. For everything that has happened. Because in spite of what Mike says now, it is my fault. Because it was my project. Everything had to be my way. And this is where we've ended up. And it's all because of me that we're here now. Hungry, cold, and hunted . . .

—Heather,
The Blair Witch Project

REASON #10 1994

Spice Girls

In 1994, a British music manager held auditions for a girl group to rival the boy bands who were dominating the charts. He was Simon Fuller (later of *American Idol* fame), and the group he formed, the Spice Girls, was an instant success. The girls were given cute nicknames—Scary Spice, Baby Spice, Sporty Spice, Ginger Spice, and Posh Spice. They strapped on platform shoes, pulled their hair up in pigtails, and told the world "what they want, what they really really want." After their first hit, "Wannabe," the girls were an unstoppable spice force. And for a few years in the '90s, it was all Spice, all the time. It ended soon, after their feature movie debut, *Spice World*. And in 1998, Ginger, aka Geri Halliwell, quit the group, leaving them just a little less spicy.

ALSO IN 1994 . . .

America Online service reaches one million members.

REASON #9   1990

Beverly Hills, 90210

Brenda and Brandon Walsh, homespun youths from Minnesota, relocate with their parents to Beverly Hills. Boy, are they in for a shock! The kids at West Beverly High are loaded—in every way. Plus, some of them are really shallow! But Brenda and Brandon acclimate, and the next thing you know, they've got a clique to call their own. Meet Kelly, Donna, Dylan, Andrea, and David, the Walshes' friends for years—and years . . . and years . . . AND YEARS! . . . to come. *90210* remained on Fox for more than a decade, taking the kids through West Beverly High, California University (Andrea Zuckerman says it's a really good school!), and into early adulthood. It made stars of the cast: the tempestuous Shannen Doherty, who ditched the role of Brenda after four seasons, Jennie Garth, Tori Spelling, Jason Priestley, Luke Perry, Brian Austin Green, and Gabrielle Carteris. And that was just the first season!

TEST YOUR *90210* KNOW-HOW

Can you match the cast member to the character he or she played?

	ACTOR		CHARACTER
1	Gabrielle Carteris	a	Gina Kincaid
2	Christine Elise	b	Brandon Walsh
3	Daniel Cosgrove	c	Scott Scanlon
4	Shannen Doherty	d	Ray Pruit
5	James Eckhouse	e	Clare Arnold
6	Douglas Emerson	f	Andrea Zuckerman
7	Mark D. Espinoza	g	Noah Hunter
8	Jennie Garth	h	Kelly Taylor
9	Brian Austin Green	i	Donna Martin
10	Vanessa Marcil	j	Brenda Walsh
11	Luke Perry	k	Dylan McKay
12	Carol Potter	l	Steve Sanders
13	Lindsay Price	m	Jesse Vasquez
14	Jason Priestley	n	Carly Reynolds
15	Kathleen Robertson	o	Cindy Walsh
16	Tori Spelling	p	Emily Valentine
17	Hilary Swank	q	Nat Buccigio
18	Joe E. Tata	r	David Silver
19	Tiffani-Amber Thiessen	s	Janet Sosna Sanders
20	Jamie Walters	t	Jim Walsh
21	Vincent Young	u	Valerie Malone
22	Ian Ziering	v	Matt Durning

Answers: 1f, 2p, 3v, 4j, 5t, 6c, 7m, 8h, 9r, 10a, 11k, 12o, 13s, 14b, 15e, 16i, 17n, 18q, 19u, 20d, 21g, 22l

REASON #8

Michael Jordan

The decade started out well for shooting guard Michael Jordan, when in 1991, he led his team, the Chicago Bulls, to their first NBA championship. It only got better from there. In the '90s, the Bulls won six championships, due largely to the prowess of Jordan, who accumulated five NBA season MVPs and six NBA Finals MVPs, and became the Bulls's all-time leading scorer, with 32,292 points at the end of his career. He was also the decade's premier endorser, appearing in nearly one hundred television commercials. Jordan hawked Hanes underwear, McDonald's Big Macs, Nike sneakers, and sports drinks by Gatorade that voiced the thought on everyone's mind: "I wanna be like Mike!"

In 1993, Michael Jordan briefly retired from basketball to pursue a lifelong dream: baseball. After a season playing minor league ball for the Birmingham Barons, he ended his baseball career and returned to the Bulls for another four years, before retiring (for good) in 1999.

REASON #7　1997

Titanic

J ames Cameron captained this historic epic about the doomed ocean liner and the rich travelers aboard it. The movie won eleven Academy Awards, including Best Picture, prompting Cameron to crow, "I'm the king of the world!" in a speech that will probably stand forever as one of Oscar's most cringeworthy moments. Kate Winslet and Leonardo DiCaprio portrayed Rose and Jack, ill-fated (and extremely good-looking) paramours from opposite worlds. Leo's sensitive portrayal of the self-sacrificing Jack made girls swoon, and the film launched Leo-mania across the country. Adding to the *Titanic* craze, the Celine Dion song "My Heart Will Go On," off the film's soundtrack, spent twenty weeks on the charts.

TITANIC WON ACADEMY AWARDS IN THE FOLLOWING CATEGORIES:

Best Picture of the Year

Achievement in Directing

Achievement in Cinematography

Achievement in Art Direction

Achievement in Sound Mixing

Original Song

Original Score

Achievement in Film Editing

Achievement in Costume Design

Achievement in Visual Effects

Achievement in Sound Editing

REASON #6   1997

Ellen DeGeneres

S he was a stand-up comedienne turned sitcom star, and in 1997, she made a public announcement that she was gay. Less than a month later, her character on her sitcom *Ellen* did the same. The coming-out episode, called "Puppy Episode," won *Ellen* a 35 percent share of the TV audience in major cities, and an Emmy Award for Writing. It was a harbinger of the new wave of gay-friendly television to come, including *Will & Grace* and *Queer Eye for the Straight Guy*.

ALSO IN 1997...

Madeleine Albright became the first woman Secretary of State.

REASON #5 — 1994

Friends

Remember when Rachel was still a waitress? When Phoebe sang "Smelly Cat"? When Joey was on *Days of Our Lives?* What about when Monica and Chandler first got together, or when Ross's first child was born?

In 1994, NBC introduced television audiences to six new friends, struggling Manhattan singles who were always between things: between jobs, between relationships, between hairstyles. In the pilot episode we made the acquaintance of siblings Monica and Ross Geller and their friends Joey, Chandler, and Phoebe. When Monica's best friend from high school showed up out of the blue, sporting a wedding dress because she'd ditched her fiancé at the altar, Monica got a new roommate, and Ross a raison d'être. Her name was Rachel, she had great hair, and wondering whether she and Ross would get together sustained the show's first season. Ross and Rachel didn't become a couple until the second season, and they'd be on again/off again for the rest of the decade—though at one point, as fans will recall, there was some confusion as to whether they were really on a break.

Jennifer Aniston's haircut—a shaggy, layered, perfectly messy do—became the most popular style of the mid-'90s. The coiff had its own name—the Rachel—and made its originator, Chris McMillan, a hairstyling star.

REASON #4

The Internet

1992: The World Wide Web is available for general use.

1994: Two graduate students start a little company called Yahoo!.

1995: The birth of Amazon.com.

1995: eBay goes live.

1996: There are 30 million internet users in the U.S.

1998: A new search engine is introduced: Google.

1999: Apple introduces the AirPort for wireless service.

REASONS THE **'90s RULED**

101

Steve Jobs, the
man behind Apple.

REASON #3

Bill Clinton

They dubbed him "the man from Hope"; he promised to fight for a "new covenant" between citizens and government; and, in 1992, along with running mate, Tennessee Senator Al Gore, he was elected the forty-second President of the United States, the first Democrat to claim the presidency since Jimmy Carter in 1976. Arkansas Governor William Jefferson Clinton, his wife, Hillary, and their daughter, Chelsea, moved into the White House in 1993; their years there were anything but dull. If it wasn't the administration's attempts to reform health care that grabbed headlines, it was Hillary's outspokenness, Chelsea's ballet recitals, or Bill's indiscretions. When Clinton was re-elected, in 1996, he became the first Democratic president since Franklin D. Roosevelt to win a second term. His tenure boasted the lowest unemployment rate and the lowest inflation in decades, plummeting crime rates, and fewer relief recipients.

In 1998, he made history again, when a sex scandal involving a robust young intern named Monica Lewinsky made him the second U.S. president to be impeached by the House of Representatives. Bill's apology to the nation went over well and he got to keep his job, living up to the nickname his adversaries gave him—"Slick Willie"—when his popular approval ratings remained intact.

> "This was not only the greatest honor of my life, but every day, even the bad days, were good days, as long as I remembered who hired me and what I was doing there."
>
> —William Jefferson Clinton

REASON #2

Nirvana

A sk Bob Dylan about being the voice of a generation (in his case, the '60s), and he'll tell you it's a farce, a burden, not something he ever wanted to be. Kurt Cobain will never be able to tell us if he found the label burdensome. As the lead singer of Nirvana—the band that not only put grunge music on the map, but without whom the entire "alternative" genre might not exist—Cobain has been called the voice of his generation ever since the release of Nirvana's first major record album, *Nevermind*.

1991's *Nevermind* was bolstered by the hit single "Smells Like Teen Spirit," which seemed to speak directly to young listeners, weaned on MTV pop, in dire need of something new. The album soared to the top of the charts, and made Nirvana (reluctant) mainstream stars. They appeared on *Saturday Night Live* and at the MTV Video Music Awards.

In 1992, Cobain married the lead singer of the band Hole—Courtney Love, who was pregnant with his child. Rumors of heroin abuse plagued the couple, who had to fight with child services to keep custody of their daughter, Frances Bean. In 1993, Nirvana released their second major-release album, *In Utero,* and Cobain's struggles with heroin addiction got worse—or at least became public. On April 5, 1994, after a failed visit to a recovery center, Cobain shot himself. He was twenty-seven years old. Fans flocked to Seattle for a candlelight vigil to mourn the loss of a musical great and Gen-X hero.

REASON #1 1990

Seinfeld

What's to say that hasn't already been said about this show about nothing? Jerry, Elaine, George, and Kramer are neurotic New Yorkers . . . yada, yada, yada. The show was the most-watched sitcom of the decade, and its much ballyhooed season finale attracted 76 million viewers . . . which sure isn't nothing.

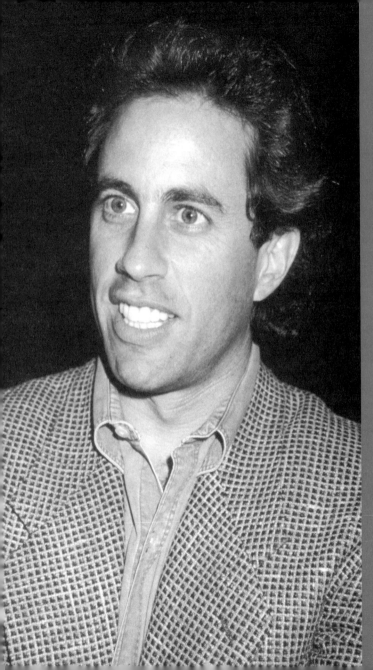

SEINFELD LEXICON

Sponge-worthy

Master of your domain

Man hands

Festivus

Not that there's anything wrong with it

Shrinkage

Soup Nazi

Close talker

Double-dipping

"I have been funny every day for nine years. It's exhausting."
—Jerry Seinfeld

ILLUSTRATION CREDITS

p. 7 Photo by ZUMA Archive/ZUMA Press. Copyright © 1994 by ZUMA Archive.

p. 10 Photo by Tim Logan/Zuma Press. Copyright © 1995 by Tim Logan.

p. 11 Photo by Jerzy Dabrowski-KPA/KEYSTONE Pictures.

p. 15 Photo by Jerzy Dabrowski-KPA/KEYSTONE Pictures. Copyright © 1998 by Jerzy Dabrowski.

p. 17 Used by permission of Warner Books. Copyright © Warner Books.

p. 19 Photo by Richard Lautens/Toronto Star/ZUMA Press. Copyright © 1991 by Richard Lautens/ Toronto Star.

p. 21 Kyle McLachlan photo by Jerzy Dabrowski-KPA/KEYSTONE Pictures. Copyright © 1998 by Jerzy Dabrowski. David Lynch photo by Terry Lilly/ZUMA Press. Copyright © 1997 by Terry Lilly.

p. 23 Ali Landry photo by Lisa O'Connor/ZUMA Press. Copyright 2001 © by Lisa O'Connor. *Gidget* photo by Nancy Kaszerman/ZUMA Press. Copyright © 1998 by Nancy Kaszerman.

p. 25 Photo by Miramax Films/ZUMA Press. Copyright © 1996 by Miramax Films. All rights reserved.

p. 27 Photo by Mike Slaughter/Toronto Star/ZUMA Press. Copyright © 1999 by Mike Slaughter/ Toronto Star.

p. 29 Photo by Jerzy Dabrowski-KPA/KEYSTONE Pictures.

p. 30 Photo by Jonathan Alcorn/ZUMA Press. Copyright © 1995 by Jonathan Alcorn.

p. 33 Photo by David Keeler/ZUMA Press. Copyright © 2001 by David Keeler.

p. 34 Photo by Frederic Injimbert/ZUMA Press. Copyright © 1994 by Frederic Injimbert.

p. 35 Photo by Frederic Injimbert/ZUMA Press. Copyright © 1994 by Frederic Injimbert.

p. 37 Photo by Jerzy Dabrowski-KPA/KEYSTONE Pictures. Copyright © 1995 by Jerzy Dabrowski.

p. 38 Photo by J.D. Beatty/ZUMA Press. Copyright © 1995 by J.D. Beatty.

p. 39 Photo by Jane Caine/ZUMA Press. Copyright © 1998 by Jane Caine.

p. 41 Photo by Steven Tackeff/ZUMA Press. Copyright © 1999 by Steven Tackeff.

p. 43 Amy Jo Johnson photo by Larry Hammerness/ZUMA Press. Copyright © 1999 by Larry Hammerness. Mighty Morphin Power Rangers photo by Saban Entertainment Inc./ZUMA Press. Copyright © 1993 by Saban Entertainment Inc. All rights reserved.

p. 45 Dan Quayle photo by Mike Clemmer/ZUMA Press. Copyright © 1989 by Mike Clemmer. Candice Bergen photo by Laura Luongo/ZUMA Press. Copyright © 1989 by Laura Luongo.

p. 47 Photo by Jerzy Dabrowsky/ZUMA Press. Copyright © 2000 by Jerzy Dabrowsky.

p. 49 Photo by Martin Philbey/ZUMA Press. Copyright © 2000 by Martin Philbey.

p. 51 Marcia Cross photo by Jane Caine/ZUMA Press. Copyright © 2003 by Jane Caine. *Melrose Place*

ACKNOWLEDGMENTS

Special thanks to E!'s Vice President of Original Programming, Betsy Rott; Executive Producer Gary Socol; and the entire *101* Production Team.